A NEW

# CHURCH

AND A NEW

# SEMINARY

DAVID MCALLISTER-WILSON

# A NEW
# CHURCH
## AND A NEW
# SEMINARY

## Theological Education
## Is the Solution

Abingdon Press
*Nashville*

A NEW CHURCH AND A NEW SEMINARY:
THEOLOGICAL EDUCATION IS THE SOLUTION

**Library of Congress Cataloging-in-Publication Data has been requested.**

ISBN: 978-1-5018-5889-5

18 19 20 21 22 23 24 25 26 27—10 9 8 7 6 5 4 3 2 1
MANUFACTURED IN THE UNITED STATES OF AMERICA

*To*
*Drema Mae McAllister-Wilson,*
*an excellent pastor, amazing woman,*
*and adored mother and grandmother.*

*And to my parents, Fred and Carol Wilson.*

# CONTENTS

# ACKNOWLEDGMENTS

I am deeply indebted to my mentors and partners in theological education: Doug Lewis, Lovett Weems, and Bruce Birch. It took a small village to produce the manuscript. Tom Berlin, Bill Gibb, Steve Lambert, and Lovett Weems exercised great patience and understanding to read successive drafts and offer comments. And I am grateful for my colleagues at Wesley who assisted me enormously as editors: Ann Michel, Carol Follett, and Josie Hoover. I am also thankful to Paul Franklyn and Neil M. Alexander at the United Methodist Publishing House for encouraging me to take on this project.

# PREFACE

I t used to be said that there were more Methodist congregations in the United States than there were post offices—at
least one in every zip code. Regardless of whether that was
literally the case, United Methodists were, and still are, one of
the most ubiquitous denominations in the United States. Like
the postal system, these congregations are the result of a complex
system of training and rapid deployment of personnel, an ability
to move capital resources wherever needed, and a shared vision of
mission and service. It's a pity to see all of that withering on the
vine. The denomination is worth saving, though not because of
what it once was or because it's too big to fail.

*The United Methodist Church is worth saving if it can serve
the present age guided by a vision of the kingdom of God, led
by the example of Jesus, and strengthened by the Holy Spirit
to make disciples of Jesus Christ who strive to make the earth
more like heaven.*

This is why I work in a United Methodist theological school.
I believe our theological schools are critical to the renewal of our
church. And, this is why I have written this book. It's rooted in
the aspirations of my seminary community—Wesley Theological
Seminary in Washington, DC. The title, *A New Church and a New
Seminary*, is taken from a case statement we developed at Wesley

to envision our future as a new kind of seminary to help renew the church. (See appendix A.)

In my first year as a seminarian, working in the development office, I was seated at a banquet next to a woman who was thought able to make a substantial contribution to Wesley Seminary: Dr. Margaret Pittman, one of the first female researchers at what became the National Institutes of Health. I spent most of the evening trying to impress her with what a great place Wesley was. She finally, politely, interrupted me: "That's fine, young man, but what are you doing about my church?" Her church, the Mount Vernon Place United Methodist Church, was a shell of its former self, as were all the formerly large downtown churches. I ended up teaching her Sunday school class for fifteen years, and now, in that church, Wesley has a satellite location and student housing. It's also where we have established our Institute for Community Engagement.[1]

Her question became one of the three defining moments in my career. The other two were 9/11, which occurred as I was transitioning to lead Wesley Seminary, and the Great Recession, which came in the seventh year of my presidency and continued for another seven—the same time arc as in the dream Joseph interpreted for Pharaoh. These events instilled in me a sense of the dramatic urgency of this moment of crisis and the determination to act decisively.

*After decades of failing to grasp the magnitude of our decline, United Methodists, including our theological schools, have finally and fully awakened to the crisis we face. This book is about how the church and its seminaries must work together to respond to this challenge.*

Betty Beene, former head of the United Way and one of my mentors, once said about both of us, "We are frequently wrong but never in doubt." She was only partially right, at least about me. I am often in doubt. But I find more is accomplished by proposing, then debating than by tentativeness. So I say some things bluntly, hoping to provoke strategic thinking and honest discussion.

This book is addressed primarily to United Methodists within the US because we have a set of issues we must resolve or we will never be the global church we aspire to be. I hope it will also be thought-provoking for those in the extended family of mainline Protestant denominations, as we are all experiencing similar challenges.

I don't speak for all thirteen United Methodist seminaries. However, all of our seminaries are part of a broad consensus within The United Methodist Church that believes we are better together than apart. I cite many examples from my seminary because I know them. But each of our seminaries has exciting and inspiring initiatives to explore.[2]

I refer to all graduate schools of theology by the generic word *seminaries*. Similarly, since those charged with leading free-standing seminaries are called "president" and "dean" if the school is related to a university, I will use the term *CEO* (Chief Executive Officer) for all of us. I alternate between the words *pastor* and *clergy*. While I understand the importance of the difference between those terms in our denomination, my intention is to speak mostly about the identified leader of congregations. Also, when I say "church" I often mean the denomination as a whole; when I say "congregation" it means a local church. But, as in the title of this book, "the church" often applies to both.

Finally, this book must address the presenting issue in my denomination, which is our bar to ordaining those people we legalistically refer to as "avowed, practicing homosexuals" and our ban on our clergy performing same-sex marriages. On the surface, our issue is homosexual practice. But I think this ignores the basic identity of millions of people. And so, I will use the acronym LGBTQ (Lesbian, Gay, Bisexual, Transgender, and Queer) to describe the people we are excluding.

As United Methodist seminary CEO, I am asked two questions that I will address here in the beginning, aiming to set them aside for at least a while.

First, what is the view of the seminaries on the church's position on LGBTQ rights? Seminary faculty differ, but I think there is some consensus. By law and the standards of academic communities, a seminary is required to practice nondiscrimination. We have spent many years trying to be inclusive communities, and we greatly value and protect all our students, regardless of sexual orientation or gender identification. But more to the point, I believe there is agreement that this focus involves a very selective use of scripture, while other issues of fidelity in sexual relationships are mentioned far more often in the Bible yet have not been raised as essential. To say nothing of the things we do or don't do, contrary to scripture, which never get discussed at General Conference.

Why have LGBTQ people become *the* issue—our Battle of Gettysburg? It's an important assumption of this book that this struggle is actually a symptom of frustration with years of membership decline, the feeling by conservatives that their values are being pushed to the margins of American culture, and the belief by both sides that this is an example of the way the church has departed from what God intends.

My view of the way forward is we require an unhappy compromise, what I would call the "annual conference option," which recognizes matters of ordination and discipline of clergy are the responsibility of the clergy in each annual conference, not the general church.

To be clear, if one of my children was in a same-gender relationship and asked me to perform the wedding, I would do so. Then I would turn in my clergy credentials. The reason I have not done this for anyone else is a mixture of cowardice and hope that we will come up with a different way to live together in this denomination.

The second question, Are there too many seminaries? Yes. And there are too many local churches and too many elders in full connection. We have too much capital tied up in our surplus of congregations while forcing new and growing churches to bear most of the cost of their mortgages or maintenance. It's just bad business and bad stewardship. But I don't have a list of which seminaries should close. In this book, I offer instead a vision for what our seminaries offer and what we must change to address the fundamental cause of the church's decline.

*There's nothing as deceptive as a problem wrongly stated. Our problem in The United Methodist Church isn't the issue of LGBTQ people. Our problem isn't even the decline in membership. Our problem isn't what we do or say as a denomination. Our problem is this: Few people outside of the clergy and lay delegates to the annual conferences care what we do or say. I want the church to matter to people in the neighborhoods of our churches across the country, to my neighborhood (Washington, DC), and to the world. And I think seminaries are a key to solving that problem.*

*Introduction*

# TO FIX MY CHURCH

The most effective church sign I ever saw was made with a Magic Marker on a bedsheet. It was draped over the fence of Fairlington United Methodist Church in Alexandria, Virginia, on September 11, 2001. A few months earlier, the church had erected a professionally built sign with The United Methodist Church's new national marketing slogan: "Open hearts. Open minds. Open doors." But it was the bedsheet announcing "Prayer service at 7:00 p.m." that drew people in.

Fairlington UMC is just two exits from the Pentagon. When the service began, the sanctuary was packed with people of all kinds. Some people had bandaged injuries. Some had seen the sign from the bus that passes the church. There were couples who had just reunited after the day's events and children who had been told the news earlier by their teachers. Longtime church members sat side-by-side in the pews with people who had never been there before. They were frightened, angry, stunned, grieving, and anxious to hear who had made it out alive.

Although she was a popular preacher, the pastor knew it was not a time to preach. Instead, there were hymns, scripture readings from the Psalms and the prophets, and prayers. When people were invited to offer public prayers, the first person to stand was the congregation's lay leader. Brian worked in the section of the

1

Pentagon destroyed by the plane. He lived to stand in the church that evening only because he happened to have been away from his office that particular morning, training the church staff in their new computer system. Those who knew wondered what he was going to say. He asked people to pray for the enemy. That prayer request was the fruit of a vital church and effective leadership. The bedsheet was a sign that a church will thrive if it meets its moment in history offering the grace of God.

I grew up in a church like that. In the 1960s, the Thousand Oaks Methodist Church in Southern California, which was a fast-growing church, full of families, very engaged in mission. We filled the new sanctuary on its very first Sunday. Pastor David Rogne was a strong and thoughtful preacher. He was known especially for delivering first-person sermons on Bible characters like Joseph, Jeremiah, Sarah, Zacchaeus, Mary, and others. He was hip. He played the Beatles' new *White Album* for the junior high Sunday school class and explained the words. And he was willing to take risks. In a very conservative all-white community full of aerospace workers, he came out for civil rights and against the Vietnam War. And the church still grew.

But after he left, the Thousand Oaks United Methodist Church began a long, slow decline. And all the pastors who followed him were blamed. Another church in our community, Calvary Community Church, met in a warehouse. They talked about the Holy Spirit and sin and salvation all the time. By the late 1970s, it had become what my church had been in the late 1960s—the strong church in town. We said it was because they were "conservative, evangelical, and fundamentalist," while we were "mainline, liberal, and ecumenical"—without ever really thinking about what any of those words might signify. Instead, we thought if we just had the right pastor, we would grow again.

I loved Thousand Oaks UMC and the people in it. My call to ministry came through these people. I still have the attendance cards they used to vote to approve me as a candidate for ministry, wrapped in red ribbon by my grandmother. Going to seminary in 1982 should have been a humbling moment, but instead I went to seminary ignorant and arrogant. I had the idea I was going to come back in three years and magically be appointed as senior pastor. I was going to fix my church.

# Seminary as Spiritual Boot Camp

Homer Dickerson, a retired minster from Nebraska, served as a volunteer chaplain at the local hospital. He would have me over to the cafeteria for breakfast to talk about going into the ministry. I still use his *Interpreter's Bible* set. He told me seminary was a place where my faith would be torn down and then built back up again (a standard warning about going to seminary). He was right, but not in the way that is usually meant.

In some significant ways, I became a Christian in seminary. Robin Gill has studied why people join churches. His research reveals that most people "belong before they believe."[1] That was me. I was a very loyal, very engaged church member. I was what I call a "legacy Christian" and what John Wesley would call an "almost Christian."[2] St. Anselm described theology as "faith seeking understanding."[3] Like many people in this secular and skeptical age, my faith journey was the reverse. It was "understanding seeking faith." Or more precisely, it was "church membership seeking faith and understanding."

I became a Wesleyan at Wesley Theological Seminary. I left behind my home church in its white suburban setting and joined the East Coast culture of Washington, DC, with its ethnic, religious, and international diversity. I interacted with students from vastly different backgrounds. I was challenged by the faculty, the courses, and all the readings. And I was inspired by a Wesleyan vision for the church as a herald and ambassador of the kingdom of God.

Seminary was the spiritual boot camp I think Homer wanted for me. I sort of expected that. I hoped I would meet someone, and I did—another seminarian. My wife, Drema, and I now have four grown children and five grandchildren. She became one of only twenty-five women pastors in the nation to lead a church of a thousand members or more. Drema was the pastor of Fairlington United Methodist Church on 9/11. She was the one who hastily wrote the invitation on the bedsheet. She is one of the best pastors I have ever encountered.

# A Church-Based Seminary

The thing I didn't expect was to work for the seminary and have theological education become my ministry. As a first-year seminarian, I worked for Wesley Seminary's new president, G. Douglass Lewis, and the new vice president, Lovett H. Weems Jr. In 1982, the seminary had been running years of deficits and, according to the auditors, was in imminent danger of closing. Doug, Lovett, and I formed a lifelong bond working together in those early years to save the seminary.

We began reading secular books on leadership to get ideas for how to turn the seminary around. Doug transformed the Board of Governors, giving a prominent role to committed lay people who brought leadership skills from their secular lives. Surprisingly, what we took from those books and those people was not a lesson in the profit motive or a corporate model of leadership. Rather, we learned how important it was to have a Moses-like focus on vision and mission, to take risks, and to have a good governance system.

From that, we determined Wesley Seminary's future depended on a closer relationship with the church. We resolved to be not just a denominationally related seminary, not merely an academic community, but a "church-based seminary." We established strong ties with surrounding annual conferences. Over time, we recruited faculty who shared this vocation. We became convinced the church could benefit, in the same way that we had, from the objective study of leadership. And so these insights are found throughout this book.

Wesley Seminary has been a good place for this kind of reflection. Doug Lewis, who retired after twenty years as president, is one of the most respected senior statesmen in theological education. He literally wrote the book on seminary presidencies.[4] Bruce Birch, who served as dean for thirteen years, wrote the book on being a seminary dean.[5] Lovett Weems went on to serve as president of Saint Paul School of Theology for eighteen years, where he orchestrated a stunning turnaround. In 2003, he returned to Wesley to build our Lewis Center for Church Leadership. Lovett is one of the most widely read authors and consultants in church leadership. Three of our faculty have gone on to lead seminaries.

# Victims of Our Own Success

In the course of this work, I also began to look at the church from a broader perspective. I realized what happened at my home congregation was happening in many others. The church had grown not only because of a particularly effective pastor but also because that pastor served the church during an era when half a million people were migrating to southern California suburbs each year, and when our town grew from 10,000 to 100,000 residents.

Many of those churches turned out to be what I think of as "mule churches." Like the sturdy pack animal, they are strong for a generation but unable to reproduce the next generation because they are sterile.

*Mule churches lack what is needed to thrive beyond a particular season and a charismatic pastor. What is most often missing is a compelling, theologically grounded, shared sense of mission and vision. This is what makes a church a driver of a community and culture rather than simply a passenger. Also missing are pastoral leaders who have the objectivity and skills to adapt to changes in the parish and the world.*

The pastors of these churches, buoyed by post-war prosperity and the baby boom, made the mistake of assuming their success was due entirely to their efforts. Psychologists and sociologists refer to these phenomena as confirmation bias and in-group bias, which are mental barriers to seeing things as they really are. Just as the demographic tide was beginning to crest, this generation of pastors became executives—district superintendents, bishops, conference staff, and members of boards of ordained ministry. Steeped in conventional wisdom, they could not see the bigger picture of what was happening or what it was going to take to adapt. Meanwhile, congregations nurtured a nostalgia for the way things were, clinging to assumptions that no longer conformed to reality.

In theory, seminaries are the solution because we are charged to produce what is needed: effective pastors with good theology. However, in the post-WWII period, seminaries also had biases. Influenced by social changes and new educational theories, we redesigned curricula and developed new models for ministry. Like golfers on a driving range at midnight with the lights out, we were swinging away without ever seeing where the ball landed— whether our techniques worked or if our graduates were effective. Seminary professors, trained primarily by academic mentors in our PhD programs, were amateurs as teachers of practitioners.

This sort of thing was happening in many American organizations, where the result was complacency and institutional momentum. And through the later decades of the twentieth century, the false sense of security in mainline Protestantism was bolstered by our economic stability. Since older members tend to give most generously, congregations didn't really feel the pinch of declining membership until the Great Recession of 2008. So too, a generation earlier, confidence in American corporations operating with no serious competition had been proven false when companies in other countries, especially Japan, rudely awakened the CEOs and shareholders and set off the alarm. This produced the first round of all those secular leadership books we read.

John Wesley may have lived too long for his own peace of mind. But he had objectivity informed by his theological vision. Near the end of his life, while others saw the growth of Methodism as a phenomenal success, he saw signs of danger. Methodists were wearing nice jewelry and spending money on fine church buildings but failing to study scripture and visit prisoners. Wesley lamented: "Does it not seem (and yet this can't be) that Christianity, true, scriptural Christianity, has a tendency, in process of time, to undermine and destroy itself?"[6] His reaction was like Moses returning to see the golden calf and smashing the tablets. He saw in the economic success of the Methodists the undisciplined self-centeredness that was so antithetical to Wesley's understanding of "true Christianity."

*Like all reformers, John Wesley tried to call the movement back to its founding principles so that it might not become a "dead sect." Today, we face a very different set of conditions, but we too are victims of our own success.*

## A Delta Moment in History

Let me offer a metaphor for this moment. The church in the US is in a "delta region" of its history. In geology, a delta is the point where a mighty river comes out of the mountains and, as the land flattens out, breaks into ever-smaller branches as it seeks the sea. The delta regions of the Tigris and Euphrates, the Nile, and the Mississippi are confusing places where boats get lost in the estuaries and flounder in the swamps. But they are also full of nutrients and life. They are the cradles of civilization. Keep both of these characteristics in mind in the following chapters.

*Some like to refer to our time as "postmodern," a concept borrowed from philosophy and art that denies the existence of inherent meaning. I prefer the delta as a way of thinking about our current confusion as a denomination, because it's a living metaphor. The delta is dangerous, and you can get lost. But it's also a fertile region. And it's hopeful because the river does find its way to the sea—even if we don't know how just now.*

What are the rules a delta boat captain uses to navigate successfully? The first is to trust the river. The old Methodist liturgy of baptism comes to mind because I memorized it by saying it so often growing up:

> The church is of God, and will be preserved to the end of time, for the conduct of worship and the due administration of God's Word and Sacrament, the maintenance of Christian fellowship and discipline, the edification of believers, and the conversion of the world.[7]

The church will be preserved to the end of time, but this isn't a promise that any particular denomination or congregation will exist that long. They won't. Our trust is the Body of Christ will persist. The psalmist says: "There is a river whose streams gladden God's city" (Ps 46:4 CEB). Our endeavor is to be a part of that river in our time—to run our course in our boat as best we can.

A delta boat captain must also change and adapt. It enhances the metaphor to know the Greek letter *delta* is used in math and physics to represent change. As Jesus says to Nicodemus: "God's Spirit blows wherever it wishes. You hear its sound, but you don't know where it comes from or where it's going. It's the same with everyone who is born of the Spirit" (John 3:8 CEB). We must be guided by our collective perception of the Spirit's movement and our sense of who we are as a people. This means we make some educated guesses about our future. The church and its seminaries are in the same boat.

# Well-Differentiated Servant Leadership

You may be thinking: leave it to a seminary CEO to use a Greek letter for an illustration. Here's another. Don't think of seminary CEOs as living in ivory towers; we stand as in a crow's nest on a ship. We have the benefit of seeing a bit farther ahead and around, as well as behind. We see a variety of churches and hear lots of different preachers and are often privy to the stories behind both their successes and their failures.

*Seminary chief executives must work in the real world. We manage people, hire and fire, and balance large budgets with multiple and shifting income streams. We deal with lawyers, accountants, and multiple bureaucracies, even as we innovate and improvise. But in our hearts, we commute to that world from a community that has a vision for what the world should be and a passionate idealism about the church. We can be useful partners, especially here, in the delta.*

We face a systemic problem, not a single issue or a certain group of people. There are some extraordinarily effective pastors who are also in the right place at the right time, and their congregations are large and/or growing. They are outliers from whom we can learn much. But the majority of pastors will never serve a church like that, and it isn't because they are lazy or incompetent. They work hard, just as much as their more successful colleagues, in very discouraging circumstances. They may not all, as the old hymn says, "preach like Peter, or pray like Paul." Few ever can. But they "tell the love of Jesus and say he died for all"[8] every week. Systemic change should focus on moving the bulge in the bell curve, the mean average. By the way, these are the pastors and churches that will suffer most if the denomination fails to stay together.

How can an unhealthy system become healthy? I have found the work of Rabbi Edwin Friedman extremely helpful in thinking about systemic problems. Many pastors and pastoral counselors are familiar with his work on family systems. Friedman also worked on larger systems, consulting with religious and military institutions, as well as for-profit and nonprofit organizations. Friedman produced a manuscript, published posthumously, describing his ultimate diagnosis of the systemic problem in our society. The book is *A Failure of Nerve: Leadership in the Age of the Quick Fix.* In it, Friedman says: "My thesis here is that the climate of contemporary America has become so chronically anxious that our society has gone into an emotional regression that is toxic to well-defined leadership."⁹

In an age when people are highly suspicious of institutions, it may seem counterintuitive to see them as an antidote to the anxiety and regression. But they are. Robert Greenleaf, one of the founding fathers of leadership studies, first coined the phrase *servant leadership.* He was convinced that this kind of leadership is usually best practiced in and through institutions. In his book *Servant Leadership: A Journey into the Nature of Legitimate Power and Greatness,* Greenleaf explains,

> Until recently, caring was largely person-to-person, now most of it's mediated through institutions—often large, complex, powerful, impersonal; not always competent; sometimes corrupt. If a better society is to be built, one that is more just and more loving, one that provides greater creative opportunity for its people, then the most open course is to raise both the capacity to serve and the very performance as servant of existing major institutions by new regenerative forces operating within them.¹⁰

Christians regularly use the phrase *servant leadership*. But it's often misapplied. A servant leader serves the mission, not the organization. Rabbi Friedman's prescription to counter our society's anxious and regressive culture applies well to the church. He calls for the cultivation of "well-differentiated leadership."

*A well-differentiated leader is committed to leading an organization but has the intellectual and emotional distance necessary to lead. A pastor is a servant of Christ and the kingdom of God, not of a congregation. I think the first task of seminaries is to prepare well-differentiated servant leaders for congregations. And we must exercise this leadership within the church ourselves.*

## Claiming the Center as Progressive Evangelicals

In the current debate about our denominational future, I am associated with a group frequently described as the "center." If "center" means "middle," that's not me. I strive to lead my institution from the center in the sense of being personally centered or in the way an athlete seeks the center of gravity. I think that's what is meant when Wesley's Way of Salvation is described as the *via media*—the middle way. Yet there's nothing halfway about it. It's more like playing center in basketball, where you claim your spot so the play can set up around you.

*Claiming the vital center involves bridging two words that usually don't go together in our current political and theological discourse: "progressive" and "evangelical." But I believe Methodists must return to thinking of ourselves as "progressive evangelicals."*

12

To be progressive is to be engaged actively in the affairs of the world, hoping and expecting that things can improve. This is why Methodists are known for our colleges and hospitals, the Salvation Army and Goodwill Industries, many hospitals, hundreds of educational institutions, and countless other efforts to foster human welfare. Progressives have an instinct to act and be on the side of those in distress and strive for inclusiveness. One reason we have experienced decline is we have forgotten we are progressive, because we fear losing members.

But we are also failing because, out of theological confusion and fear of embarrassment, we have forgotten we are evangelical. To be an evangelical is to believe in a personal God, one who is concerned with our whole being, one on whom we can call as a child calls out to a parent. It means we come to know Jesus as a friend, we believe in his resurrection, and we believe in the ever-present, personal power of the Holy Spirit to redeem our lives and transform the world.

What connects our identity as progressives and as evangelicals is our belief in a personal God who expects things of each of us personally. Methodists believe the good news is the kingdom of God. And we believe God wants no one left behind. We don't just believe these things; we proclaim them and practice them. Methodism is spirituality with an attitude and an agenda.

## Changing Our Value Proposition

Here is an illustration of what needs to change in order for us to become new again. In most of our churches, the function of the evangelism committee is to recruit new members. This implies that the evangel, the gospel or the good news, is something like this: "We have a great church here, and if you join, you will have a better life." But here's the good news according to Jesus: "After John was arrested, Jesus came into Galilee announcing God's good news, saying, 'Now is the time! Here comes God's kingdom! Change your hearts and lives, and trust this good news!'" (Mark 1:14-15 CEB).

Belonging to a local fellowship of Christians is essential to introduce people to Jesus Christ and help them begin to live as citizens of the kingdom of God. But when we conflate evangelism with joining the church, we end up equating the church with the kingdom and membership with discipleship. And the way we finance our churches—treating them as clubs with dues-paying members—isn't only a theological problem, it's just not working as it once did for the majority of churches. This is how a church turns into a mule.

We need to reconsider what people in the business world would call our "value proposition." We have, inadvertently, turned a march to Zion into a trip to an increasingly deserted shopping mall stocked with things people don't want to buy. Our experience and research tells us this approach has produced diminishing returns, not just with millennials but also with baby boomers. The problem is, like Sears stores in the 1970s, we are invested so heavily in the member-services model of church that it's hard for us to imagine any other sustainable model. One of the essential roles of theological education is to remember we were once not like we are now and to dream of how we could be.

Methodists have adapted our business model before. David Hempton's *Empire of the Spirit* is a history of the expansion of Methodism. He describes how we were able to change our structure because we were "an ecclesiology based on the principle of association." Hempton explains,

> Even during Wesley's lifetime, but more commonly afterward in both Britain and America, there were fierce debates within Methodism about who had the right to make the rules, what the rules should be, and how they should be enforced. These are essentially preoccupations of a voluntary association, not of a confessional church.... Over time, it invented tradition to suit the current needs of the inventors.[11]

*I believe The United Methodist Church can reinvent ourselves again. And it's time to make some decisions with a coalition of the willing rather than waiting hopelessly for unanimity. I went to seminary to fix my church. That was a particular congregation. Now I see that the health of particular congregations and their ability to be a part of a bigger mission requires a healthy denomination. I'm still in seminary to fix the church. But I realize now that it is going to require a new seminary for a new church.*

# IT'S JUST NOT
# WORKING ANYMORE

T om Berlin is the chair of Wesley Theological Seminary's
Board of Governors. When he's frustrated, he says: "It's
just not working anymore." Tom is pastor of Floris
UMC, located in a Virginia suburb of Washington, DC. Floris is
one of the one hundred largest United Methodist churches in the
US. Tom is always among the first clergy elected to represent the
Virginia Annual Conference at General Conference, and he serves
on the Commission on the Way Forward (a group tasked with
finding a solution to the dispute that could divide United Methodist polity). Tom as an optimistic, articulate, thoughtful pastor
who calls out the best in others and very much wants to fix the
church. Think of him as our Tom Hanks. (He even looks like the
guy who plays the part of the sun on the Jimmy Dean Breakfast
Sandwich commercial). So, when Tom says, "It's just not working
anymore," his discouragement is discouraging. Tom isn't alone.

> *Leaders in all quarters of our denomination are reaching
> the same conclusion: it's just not working anymore. I get it in
> the form of questions from students and prospective students
> who ask, "What am I getting into?" "Will I be able to stay in
> ministry if I pay for this degree?"*

# Can We Restart Our Movement?

Through the ages, most people became Christians without thinking much about it. They joined because other people did—their tribal chief or monarch, their parents, their neighbors, their spouse, or even their children. For decades, this type momentum fueled the growth of our congregations. But when it stops working, it's like running out of gas at the bottom of the hill.

In a movement, most people believe in the cause. In an institution, most people believe in the institution. Movements beget institutions. This is what happened to us. But institutions also beget movements. In China today, Christianity is a fast-moving movement. Nearby in Korea, which has the largest Methodist congregations in the world, churches have reached an amazing degree of institutional development and are now thinking about how to foster new movements. I believe The United Methodist Church in the US is in "late-stage institutionalism," and the question is whether we can restart the movement again.

*Two groups have the biggest influence on whether we can become a movement again: (1) appointed and elected denominational leaders and (2) the leaders of our theological schools. These two groups must come to a consensus about the gravity of our condition and the importance of reviving the movement.*

## Indicators of Systemic Failure

I could spend every Sunday for a year attending worship in a thriving United Methodist congregation in the mid-Atlantic area. But they are like pools of water in a drying riverbed.

18

Our denomination is experiencing the psychological and social equivalent of an economic recession. And, as with an economic recession, the problem is system-wide. What are the signs? Let me begin with some of the more objectively verifiable signs of systemic failure:

1.  A steady decline in church membership and worship attendance despite an increase in the overall population.[1]

2.  A continual increase in the average age of our congregations, compared to the general population.

3.  Our inability to plant many truly successful new churches or to close enough old, unsuccessful churches.

4.  Our failure to attract enough young, diverse, and high-quality new clergy, and our inability to remediate or remove poorly performing clergy.

Additionally, there are some more subjective signs of systemic failure:

1.  Increasingly, some of our best pastors are reluctant to be nominated to the episcopacy, and bishops find it harder to recruit them to serve as district superintendents. And, year after year, the same individuals seem to be re-elected as lay delegates to annual conferences.

2.  Fewer of the best college students from strong church backgrounds express an interest in ministry as a profession, and many of those who do enter seminary say they want something other than the local church ministry.

3.  For some time, in many churches, the average amount

given by individual members has been on the rise because fewer people are giving larger gifts. This is the heroic efforts of the most loyal, often older members to counteract a shrinking donor base.

4. Our General Conference has been transfixed for more than twenty years by the continued disagreement over the acceptance of LGBTQ people. This is a symptom of something broken in the body politic. As a longtime resident of Washington, DC, I recognize the pattern of polarization and legislative gridlock.

We have earnestly tried to reverse many of the trends. We have spent considerable time and money with little or no result, even though we are full of good, smart, well-meaning people. A team that's working really well is said to be "more than the sum of its parts." Conversely, a team that isn't working well is "less than the sum of its parts." Isn't that the case with us?

In 2012, Lovett Weems introduced the riveting metaphor of the "death tsunami." His book *Focus: The Real Challenges That Face The United Methodist Church*,[2] published in advance of the 2012 General Conference, presented research documenting the aging of our denomination. Most people can see that with their own eyes on any given Sunday morning. But what's not as apparent to people in the pews is that this trend is accelerating. The projection shows a veritable tidal wave of deaths, cresting sometime between 2040 and 2050. While the United States population is aging, it's dramatically more so in the church. So not only is it "just not working anymore"—it's going to get worse. (I would have added that in the title of this chapter, but it sounded too grim.)

# Price Point: The Challenge for Seminaries

What about our theological schools? A well-known business school came to me several years ago exploring the possibility of a joint degree. They had developed a "product," as they called it. It was an MBA for the social sector, where they had forged a partnership with a medical school to prepare hospital administrators. Now they thought clergy might be a vast untapped market. After a few rounds of conversation, they broke it off, saying, "There's no money in educating clergy." This was an epiphany for a business school dean but a reality I deal with daily.

> *The precise problem seminaries face is what marketers would call the "price point." The salary churches are willing to pay pastors, and the amount they are willing to contribute through the church for their education, isn't commensurate with the level of education they require of clergy. In fields such as medicine, law, or architecture, the level of professional salaries supports the cost of professional education. But the starting salaries of pastors are significantly lower than the starting salaries in these other professions. And clergy never catch up.*

All the schools in the Association of Theological Schools in the US and Canada (ATS) are experiencing unparalleled challenges. A few years ago, Daniel Aleshire, then head of the ATS, said that a third of the ATS's 276 seminaries were in severe financial difficulty. My experience of eight years on the United Methodist University Senate tells me the figure is much higher than that. We are facing a perfect storm of reduced tuition and gift revenue, rising student debt, and a questioning of the value proposition of higher education.

21

Almost all seminaries of all denominations have made significant cuts since the beginning of the Great Recession in 2008. Some of the wealthiest schools disclosed significant reductions in faculty and programs in the long wake of the recession.[3] Many have had to draw down reserves and take even more drastic action in search of financial stability.

# The Return on Investment for United Methodist Seminaries

What about the thirteen United Methodist seminaries? We are a good investment for the denomination. We are consistently considered among the highest quality schools in the ATS, and seven United Methodist seminaries are among the forty wealthiest ATS schools, as measured by long-term investments.[4] The United Methodist seminaries with PhD programs supply a large portion of the faculty and texts for other schools. We prepare the majority of United Methodist elders, and that share is increasing. Moreover, we return substantially more to the denomination than we receive in preferential scholarships for United Methodist students, in preferential hiring of United Methodist faculty, and through support of the Course of Study and central conference theological education.

The way seminaries have made it work thus far is to try to keep costs down relative to the rest of higher education. Student housing at Wesley Seminary, for instance, costs only half as much as it does at the United Methodist–related American University next door. Senior administrator salary levels are significantly lower than counterparts in higher education. All of our seminaries discount already low tuition rates with scholarship funds drawn from money we raise.

Since 1968, The United Methodist Church's Ministerial Education Fund (MEF) has been one of the most important sources of revenue for seminaries. The MEF is one of seven "general church funds" that are funded by collections from congregations and annual conference reserve funds, and they are annually distributed by denominational offices for various church-wide causes. Of the amount collected for the MEF, 56 percent makes its way to the thirteen seminaries.[5] It's divided among us according to a formula that is weighted based on the number of certified candidates for ministry enrolled and the success record of each seminary's graduates in completing ordination. There is also a preferential portion given to schools with PhD programs. Faculties in MEF-supported schools must include a substantial portion of tenured professors from the denominations in the World Methodist Council. When the MEF was established, it helped our schools develop to become among the best theological schools in North America. The MEF fund is still critical for us, but it's a shrinking percentage of our total budgets because general church apportionments have not kept pace with inflation.

So the heads of our theological schools have become relentless fundraisers. Because the majority of our alumni are clergy with low salaries and obligations to raise money for their own congregations, most of our gifts come from individuals who have never taken a class at our schools.

In some cases, seminaries raise significant grant income for projects in research and development. And we have become marketers, especially in our efforts to recruit non–United Methodist students and students in new kinds of degree and nondegree programs. The tuition from these programs helps subsidize the United Methodist students enrolled in the master of divinity degree. However, the return on investment for our marketing dollars is poor because of the low price point. And our nondegree programs are constrained because the economics of continuing education are different for clergy. Other professionals have employers who pay for executive education, or they pay out of their pocket, knowing their education will increase earnings down the road.

Similarly, the price congregations are willing to pay for high-quality adult education materials doesn't cover the cost of their production. Nevertheless, every one of our seminaries donates faculty time for a myriad of lay education opportunities.[6]

*Through our fundraising, grant-writing, and marketing efforts, the thirteen United Methodist seminaries bring in large amounts of financial resources from beyond the denomination to pay for the preparation of United Methodist clergy in the US and for other services to the church. And we provide the second largest source of funds for the preparation of United Methodist clergy outside the US. What other United Methodist organization is producing such a large net return on investment to the denomination?*

The other way we have been making it work is through debt financing, and it's the students who have borne that debt. I'm not nearly as worried about my one son's $400,000 university and medical school debt or another son's $250,000 mortgage as I am about the many United Methodist seminary students incurring over $40,000 in student loans, which currently bear interest rates of 6 percent and higher. This can't continue.

# Is a Voucher System the Answer?

Every four years, a populist sentiment raises the possibility of turning the MEF into a voucher system, distributing it directly to United Methodist students. There are three reasons this is a bad idea.

1.  A voucher program could only be offered to certified candidates for ordained ministry. But many students don't decide to seek ordination until they are well into their seminary education.

2.  A voucher program would be administered through annual conferences, which already administer 25 percent of the apportioned MEF funds. But some annual conferences don't have good records of accountability administering MEF funds. The conferences would have to add professional staff to administer the vouchers, creating more overhead.

3.  Vouchers would drive up the cost to students in the same way government-guaranteed student loans have driven up costs in the overall educational market. Some United Methodist students would use their vouchers to go to the lower-quality but more convenient non–United Methodist seminary. This would save some of the weakest and most financially distressed seminaries in the industry. They would raise their tuition rates without offering preferential financial assistance to United Methodist students. Simultaneously, the United Methodist seminaries, who do now offer preferential scholarships, would have to raise tuition rates and cut financial aid. Why would we rent space in seminaries not interested in the future of our movement when we own space in our own schools?

# Theological Schools Have Reached a Tipping Point

Theological schools have worked hard to remain competitive. Competition can be a good thing. When these economic incentives work in the same direction as our mission, they can produce powerful results. Competitive pressure has produced creative new programs and effective administrators. We have become more in touch with the issues of the church than seminaries not affiliated with a denomination have.

However, some of our seminaries are teetering on the brink of viability. All of us are raising funds from the same shrinking base of mainline Protestant lay people and a small pool of foundations interested in religion. But perhaps the most toxic trend is the heavy competition between sister schools for young applicants with high GPAs. For example, to stay in this game, Wesley Seminary has had to increase financial aid by reducing funds for other vital areas. Some of our schools are running significant deficits in their operating budgets and exhausting their resources. Others are selling or abandoning their campuses and seeking partnerships and mergers in order to survive. The truth is, we are accepting some students who have little chance to be effective pastors, and we are in danger of degrading the quality of our educational programs.

So how are our seminaries doing? Recall the business school dean's revelation: "There's no money in educating clergy." While we aren't in it for the money, we can only continue to serve within a viable economic framework.

# End-Stage Institutionalism

One of the most influential leadership gurus of our time is Jim Collins. He is best known for his book *Good to Great: Why Some Companies Make the Leap...and Others Don't.*[7] Just before the beginning of the Great Recession of 2008 he published an even more helpful book, *How the Mighty Fall: And Why Some Companies Never Give In.* This book examines seemingly strong corporations, including some Collins had labeled "great" a decade earlier, which did not remain great. Collins describes five stages of the fall:

1. Hubris born of success

2. Undisciplined pursuit of more

3. Denial of risk and peril

4. Grasping for salvation

5. Capitulation to irrelevance or death[8]

The critical thing to notice about the stages of failure is the way success prevents us from accurately perceiving the decline. This is what happened to my home church, and this is what John Wesley feared as the Methodist movement became more established. Think of the churches and annual conferences that responded to obvious signs of long-term decline by building new buildings or engaging in ambitious capital campaigns—trying to "dress for success" instead of facing hard truths.

In a leadership course I teach, I ask pastors, "What stage is your church in?" and "What stage is your denomination in?" In general, the more successful and seasoned pastors see themselves at greater peril. This is because effective leaders have good situational awareness and a willingness to make honest assessment. For example, even though we marvel at the size of the Methodist churches in South Korea, when I ask them to score their churches, they are now more likely to realize their churches are in danger than they were able to admit ten years ago. United States pastors in my class typically see their congregations between Stage 2 (undisciplined pursuit of more) and Stage 3 (denial of risk and peril). They are less generous in their assessment of the state of the denomination, rating it between Stage 3 (denial of risk and peril) and Stage 4 (grasping for salvation).

> *If we were a sports team, it would be time for a coaching change. But there is no coach. And there is no headquarters— as I sometimes finding myself explaining to incredulous CEOs from other fields—and, unless or until we face a bankruptcy judge, there won't be. There is no single steering wheel, so we must find ways to act with the assistance of grace and mutual sacrifice.*

Now is the time to choose whether we want to work together or split. We agree there is a problem, but there isn't a unity that our unity matters, that The United Methodist Church is worth saving because our bonds are precious, our shared vision is righteous, and we accomplish more together than we could apart.

The search for unity is producing diminishing returns as positions become more entrenched. Paradoxically, the effort has become counterproductive as we have spiritualized our politics. Calling something "holy conferencing," when it's really lobbying or a negotiating strategy, deafens us to the actual voice of God.

Instead, we must seek a consensus rather than unity to move forward. We must then make some very tough decisions and uninspiring compromises, which will not feel very "holy" until long

28

after they are made. And, as we do, let's picture Jesus on neither side; he stands equidistant and weeping, beckoning us to a different future.

## Are Seminaries Part of the Problem?

I've shared some brutal facts and blunt criticism. In that same vein, it's fair to ask, are the United Methodist theological schools part of the problem? Are we part of the reason "it just isn't working anymore"? When I entered seminary in 1982, it was common for people in the church to say that theological schools were elitist. And back then, there was some truth in that criticism.

This is the kind of criticism we heard as we began to reinvent Wesley Seminary. Rightly or wrongly, we were seen as part of the problem. Our approach was to become what we call a "church-based seminary." Similar changes have been made at each of our United Methodist seminaries. We differ from one another because we reflect the different nature of the churches in our various regions; yet each of us is providing creative and adaptive leadership, though some are struggling to maintain financial viability.

Still, many ask whether advanced, professional theological education is worth the investment. It's fair to observe that the master of divinity has only become the norm for full-time pastoral ministry in the last eighty years and that membership in mainline Protestant churches has declined seemingly in lockstep. Is there a connection?

Some historical perspective is important. First, studies of theological education going back to the 1920s report concern about both the quality of candidates coming to seminary and complaints from the church regarding those entering the ministry.[9] However, at every period of challenge in the two-thousand-year history of the church, it has elected to increase the level of education required of its clergy. This is especially true in those times when the quality of the clergy is seen to be lagging behind the increasing education of the laity and the complexity of society.

This same pattern is at work today. Within Methodism, for instance, just as The United Methodist Church is seeing a decrease in the percentage of clergy receiving the master of divinity degree, the central conferences, the African Methodist Episcopal Church, and the Korean Methodist Church are encouraging greater levels of education for their clergy. Outside the denomination, the greatest demand for seminary training is in the fastest-growing church in the world, China.

*Many bishops and boards of ordained ministry complain about the quality of some of the candidates they are seeing. In return, the seminaries point out that these candidates came from their churches, often with enthusiastic recommendations from these same officials. We all have a mutual stake and a shared responsibility for the quality of clergy we ultimately train, ordain, and appoint.*

## Are Seminaries Too Liberal?

While working on this book, I spent a few days in William Gladstone's library in Wales, United Kingdom. Gladstone was one of the most influential British prime ministers and led four governments under Queen Victoria. He was an extremely religious and conservative man, first a Tory (Conservative), then head of the Liberal Party, which I mention to point out that the meaning of the words *liberal* and *conservative* shift with circumstance. I was nestled in the most comfortable chair I could find, deep in Gladstone's book stacks, trying to answer this question about whether seminary faculty are too liberal. Don't be impressed with my scholarship—I was there for the chair—but I happened to glance up at the books at eye level on the shelf and saw a title: *Liberalism in Religion*, by William Page Roberts, prominent Anglican clergyman at the end of the nineteenth century. I grabbed it and opened to a random page, and the first sentence I read puts best what I want to say: "Liberalism *in* religion is Conservativism *of* religion. If it were not, I would not be its apologist."[10]

Are seminary faculty too liberal? I imagine a majority of them voted for the Democrat in the last several presidential elections. On average, they tend to be on the liberal side of a range of issues, although less so than academics in secular schools. They are also liberal in the sense of believing in free speech and intellectual inquiry. And they know the Old and New Testaments have a developmental history and contain inconsistencies, which are meant to be explored, unafraid.

On the other hand, as scholars, they are inherently conservative of the texts and traditions of the faith. They know the Bible better than anyone and read it in the original languages. They are men and women of principled character. They experience their work in a seminary as a call of God. Why else would someone spend so much time and money on an otherwise useless degree? They are committed to the church by vocation and are critics by profession. They put their students first. Most go to their churches every Sunday, except for the many times they are preaching or teaching elsewhere. The most meaningful time for our faculty at

Wesley Seminary is the worship service before commencement, when they lay hands on and pray for the graduating seniors.

*If you define* liberal *as open and believing in the importance and possibility of progress toward a peaceful and just society, then yes, seminary faculties are liberal. They are liberal just as John Wesley was more liberal than his contemporaries, just as the Salvation Army was more liberal than the rest of Methodism in its day, and just as Korean Methodists and West African Methodists are more liberal than the other faiths in those contexts.*

But what people often really mean when they ask if seminary faculty are liberal is "Are they out of touch with the church?" In short, the answer is no. In addition to the churches they regularly attend and the ones they visit, they hear students and alumni speak about the reality of their churches. They are in touch with a greater number and greater variety of churches than most pastors who know only the few churches they serve.

Seminary faculty are, however, often idealistic, unrealistic, and impractical, as any seminary CEO will attest. But don't we need them to be? To borrow a term from British politics, seminary faculty should be the loyal opposition to the established church because they have a passion for what the church is meant to be. They don't think about whether what they teach is marketable or even whether it preaches next Sunday. They are concerned with what is true in the sense of being accurate as well as true like a compass, pointing toward the more excellent way.

I will have more to say about how seminaries must change. But the problem isn't that our faculties are too liberal. They are not the cause of the decline of the church. They are part of the solution.

# Focus on the Future

Let's look at what has happened from a different perspective. Consider the extraordinary changes happening in the US over the last generation. In 1955, the year I was born, 50 percent of households were married couples with children in the home. Today, that demographic is 20 percent. During that same period, the ethnic and religious diversity of the country has increased substantially. United Methodist churches have been struggling to adapt to these dramatic changes to their traditional base. Also, we have watched the culture become secularized. The evidence is trivial but telling. On Sunday mornings, kids are in soccer at 11:00; the only businesses not open are dry cleaners; and pastors no longer receive free membership in country clubs. We should have adapted better to changes in the culture signified by these examples. But those mistakes are in the past.

*Have you ever been in a traffic jam that goes for miles and finally opens up, but you never see what caused it? Those who study traffic and other moving systems say this lag time is a common feature. What we are experiencing now isn't the fault of anyone currently caught up in our system. Whatever went wrong went wrong some years ago. Now we must set our sight back on Jerusalem.*

# WHY IT MATTERS

## Methodism as an Experiment in Grace

Why does it matter that we stay together as Methodists? Those of us who seek to remain united and seek compromise on the issues of inclusion of LGBTQ people share a feeling that separation isn't good for us and isn't what God intends. It's like the desire to avoid breaking up a marriage or a family. We have a theological instinct about this "centrist" position. But it isn't always explicitly articulated.

So why does it matter? Often we answer talking about our "connectionalism" as a covenant, or how we are "organized for mission," or that we are "open and inclusive." But that places form over function. Let me illustrate the importance of the distinction by looking at an example of the difference between *religion* and *faith*.

Soon after the attacks on 9/11, I got a call from a friend at the Central Intelligence Agency. He was part of a group of analysts who had developed a model to assess the stability of a country. They realized their model included religion as a social criterion like sports and fashion, rather than as a primary motivating factor for non-state actors. So they asked me to assemble a group of professors to help them think about how to improve their predictions.

We talked with the analysts about lived religion—faith understood through what was being taught, preached, or prayed for—because this would inform what was shaping the hopes and fears of a significant number of Muslims (or Christians, Jews, Hindus, Buddhists, to name a few).

What is our lived religion as United Methodists? Earlier I characterized us as "progressive evangelicals." There are other ways to say it. Lovett Weems uses the phrase "an evangelical church in a liberal tradition."[1] In an address to the Council of Bishops in 2007, he asked if such a combination could thrive:

> Could this Wesleyan identity be captured in an inclusive vision of an evangelical church in a liberal tradition? We are an evangelical church. At the same time, we are in a liberal tradition. We are the first to challenge assumptions. We are the first to open windows and doors to new ideas and possibilities when faith mandates it. Could such a vision that is both deep (in faith and piety) and open (to new needs and possibilities) sustain us over the years ahead?[2]

*An inclusive Methodist theology of unity is grounded in a belief that we, as proponents of grace, are in a covenant that is personal and transformational, not legal and transactional. "Church trials" are anathema to the spirt of Methodism. We should not exercise that kind of "authority" over each other.*

With the same reason, I say to liberals we are simultaneously "evangelical" as well as "progressive." David Hempton, Dean of Harvard Divinity School, described us well:

If Wesley's theology must be reduced to a model, one that offers better explanatory power than the quadrilateral is to see it more as a moving vortex, fueled by scripture and divine love, shaped by experience, reason, and tradition and moving dynamically toward holiness or Christian perfection. Any model that lacks dynamic movement toward holiness and its growth within individuals and its dissemination throughout the world is clearly inadequate.[3]

# Our Genetic Legacy

Living things thrive over time if they adapt and yet stay true to a basic identity. Just as a fun thought experiment, think of Dorothy's musical question in *The Wizard of Oz*:

If happy little bluebirds fly...
why, oh why, can't I?

Well, why can't humans fly? It's because the human gene pool just doesn't have the necessary set of conditions to morph in this direction. So we are left to adapt within the limits of humankind. The scientific phrase is *evolutionary constraints*.

We should think about our evolutionary constraints as United Methodists, because so many pastors and congregations feel like they are being asked to sprout wings and fly to the moon. Instead, they should strive to be their best selves. When large churches have successful church plants, they speak of transmitting the mother church's DNA. We should be guided by our instinctive theological wisdom even as we adapt in order to stay true to our best selves. Or, as Dorothy put it, "There's no place like home." A primary responsibility of our denominational seminaries is to remind us what "home" is.

So what is the genetic legacy of Methodism? Some have recently asserted that it's biblical authority. One feels vaguely unpatriotic to argue against that. Of course, we take the Bible normatively, but John Wesley's own approach to scripture is instructive. He applied an overarching interpretive framework, which he called the "analogy of faith." He saw a deep pattern to everything in scripture that corresponded to his understanding of the process of salvation. As Randy Maddox points out, Wesley "required that all passages be read in light of these truths."[4] Wesley thought this was the correct way to understand scriptural texts and believed his analogy of faith conformed to the historic creeds of the church. Yet it still is a method of filtering, sorting, and prioritizing scripture. Biblical authority was, for early Methodists, part of a larger theological project.

Others, often in the opposite camp, see the essential principle of Methodism in John Wesley's tolerance of theological difference, his "catholic spirit." An example of that is found early in the history of the movement when he said: "But as to all opinions which don't strike at the root of Christianity, we think and let think. So that whatsoever they are, whether right or wrong, they are no distinguishing marks of a Methodist."[5] Many liberals like to cite Albert Outler's formulation of the Wesleyan quadrilateral: "scripture, tradition, reason, and experience." (I suspect some of the attraction of the quadrilateral is because you can pick any one of these, especially reason or everyday experiences, to trump scripture or tradition.) The problem with these approaches is the same problem with The United Methodist advertising slogan, "Open Hearts. Open Minds. Open Doors." Just to say we are open doesn't say why people would care to come in.

# Methodism Is an Experiment in Grace

I suggest the essence of Methodism is found in what John Wesley calls our "doctrine and discipline." Observe how he uses these words in the following passage expressing his fear about the future of the movement:

> I am not afraid that the people called Methodists should ever cease to exist either in Europe or America. But I am afraid lest they should only exist as a dead sect, having the form of religion without the power. And this undoubtedly will be the case, unless they hold fast both the doctrine, spirit, and discipline with which they first set out.[6]

The meaning of those words takes some interpretation because, at first, it seems like a stern and inflexible charge. Of course, when he says *discipline,* he doesn't mean *The Book of Discipline.* And, although we would refer to him today as an "obsessive" man, his use of the word *doctrine* doesn't mean we are to be doctrinaire. Wesley ardently defends himself as upholding all the doctrines of the church. But when he does that, it strikes me as tactical. He was resisting those who were accusing him of having no norms (antinomian) precisely because he was vulnerable to such a criticism in his attempt to discover a subjective path to what he called "real Christianity."

However, I believe what Wesley meant by those terms is, in fact, our distinctive inheritance. But in place of "doctrine and discipline," think "method." We are convinced that God is active in our lives, even beyond our knowledge of it and regardless of merit. This is grace. And John Wesley hoped we would evidence the power of grace rather than the mere form of religion. That power, to use the archaic language every Methodist seminarian learns, functions as "prevenient, justifying, and sanctifying grace." I find it helpful to think of those movements as the "pervasive, transformative, and progressive" effects of the Holy Spirit.

In the words of Charles Wesley's hymn, we "seek a principle within,"[7] and our method is accountable discipleship. It's helpful to picture the early Methodist class meetings as being much more like the addiction support group that rents a Sunday school classroom than any of the other fellowship groups that are meeting in the church that week. Accountable discipleship is a disciplined and communal approach to discovering, nurturing, and sharing the experience of the Holy Spirit in our lives.

Isn't this conviction of the immediacy of the Holy Spirit, and the belief that our primary task is to grow in grace and extend that grace to the world, the essence of who we are as Methodists? Isn't this in our evolutionary constraint, the dominant gene in our DNA that relates all the descendants of Methodism who have evolved to fit their time and place?

John Wesley, in his sermon "The Good Steward," thought of us as stewards—caretakers—of the "grace of God, the power of his Holy Spirit, which alone worketh in us all that is acceptable in his sight."[8] Randy Maddox calls it responsible grace, and Tom Langford (following John's mother, Susanna Wesley) calls it practical divinity.[9] And the purpose is our distinctively audacious view that we are actually working out our own salvation, as John Wesley said. And we are progressing and going on to perfection.

You could say, to borrow a phrase from the Gettysburg Address, we are "dedicated to the proposition" of grace. But it's more helpful to say we are testing a theory. In the early part of our movement, the proposition of grace had a status like that of a scientific hypothesis, constantly being tested and verified. John Wesley was part of the dawn of modern science, fascinated by all the new discoveries about the way the physical world works. This appears throughout his journals, and his most financially success-ful publication was a book of medical advice: *Primitive Physick: Or an Easy, Natural Method of Curing Most Diseases.*[10] "Experimenting," and "experiencing" described the same activity in the eighteenth century.

Just as John Wesley's contemporary Benjamin Franklin made the connection between the power of lightning from the heavens and electrical phenomena on earth, Wesley and the members of the Holy Club were conducting experiments on the other power emanating from heaven—the grace of God—and how that power can be experienced. Had he known of the per-vasiveness of electricity, even to the cellular and atomic level, he would have found an even more robust analogy of his hypothesis that grace is infused in and drives all creation. Methodists, and all our aunts and uncles and cousins, are a longitudinal study in the experience of God's power to transform lives individually and in community.

*Methodism, at its heart, is an experiment in grace. It's a method for spiritual development that became an extensive and massive institution. Though we have become highly so-lidified in our form, we are experimental and adaptive in our nature and function. To return to Lovett Weems's formula, because we seek the real presence of the Holy Spirit, we are "deep"; because we are an experiment in grace and look for its urgings everywhere, we are "open."*

# A Spirituality for Crisis

Earlier, I described Rabbi Friedman's diagnosis of our society as chronically anxious. Methodism is, distinctively, a "spirituality" for this kind of existential crisis. I put that word *spirituality* in quotation marks because I can't think of a better word, even though it is losing its meaning by overuse. "Spirituality of" has become a preface for every possible activity, condition, and inanimate object.

Christianity is a spirituality that emanates from the life, death, and resurrection of Jesus of Nazareth and the in-breaking of the kingdom of God. It's a compass that reads true in all circumstances. Methodism is at heart a discipline to check that compass often—a spiritual discipline particularly suited for personal, social, and intellectual delta regions of existential confusion and crisis.

*To put it plainly, Methodism is a lived religion only if those who have little or no faith, including those who are done with religion, are experiencing the Holy Spirit and lack only the way to know it for what it is.*

I confess a personal discomfort with the word *spirituality*. We use the vocabulary of feelings and emotions when we talk about describing a relationship with God. When I read the very popular book *The Five Love Languages: How to Express Heartfelt Commitment to Your Mate*[11] I was not surprised to discover my love language is acts of service. It would be easier for me to extract my own wisdom tooth than talk about feelings. I'm Martha, my wife is Mary. (Her love language is words of affirmation.) And I know Jesus likes her better.

Nevertheless, I must give a personal account, because the Methodist experiment in grace is only validated by experience. This is the meaning of 1 John 4:1, "Dear friends, don't believe every spirit. Test the spirits to see if they are from God because many false prophets have gone into the world" (CEB).

I was once satisfied that the best way to speak about spirituality in Methodism was to stay in the broad lane of sanctifying grace. There, we speak of the Spirit assisting us to grow. It's easy to say God wants to help us make spiritual progress. We can talk church program as thought it's physical exercise with grace as the rush of religious endorphins. But if people want only that, they can go to a gym and play Gregorian chants through their earbuds. Frankly, they don't need a church for that. It doesn't speak to the depth of human need nor the height of our longing.

Instead, if we accept our full theological inheritance, it helps us get to the real issues of human existence—the big questions about the meaning of life and death, sin and salvation.

How do Methodists look at these questions? It's necessary to set the stage with some technical terms. In his book *Responsible Grace: John Wesley's Practical Theology*, Randy Maddox concludes Wesley started "amillenialist, flirted with premillenialism and ended up postmillienialist because it fit well with his progressive eschatology."[12] This simply means we believe we live in a time when God is particularly active, urging, enticing, beguiling us to engage in the great personal drama of creation and salvation. To use Jesus's words for it, "Change your hearts and lives! Here comes the kingdom of heaven!" (Matt 3:2 CEB).

# What Do You Fear?

Right from the start, I found myself in a crisis of faith in my first semester in the course Methodist History and Doctrine. We were studying the Methodist understanding of salvation, and I encountered the simple entrance requirement to the early Methodist Society. One had *only* to have "the desire to flee the wrath to come; to be saved from our sins." People flocked to the meetings out of the experience of guilt for sins and fear of eternal damnation. What's more, Methodists understood that this experience was, itself, God at work, which explains the piece of the hymn *Amazing Grace* that is incomprehensible for many today: " 'Twas grace that taught my heart to fear."

Strange, I thought, that grace would teach fear so as to accomplish salvation. It felt like I was back in my youth director days because I was hearing again the language of the local Baptist church and Calvary Community Church in my hometown. These are the churches we called "evangelical" in a dismissive way. But now I realized, Methodists are evangelicals. And they talk about feelings!

The crisis was a secret I kept to myself for a long time because I felt like a fraud. I never had that experience. I was not afraid of eternal torment. And candidly, while some people I know fear the wrath to come, many others don't. However, Lester Ruth, whose research is in the history of Christian worship, explains something I find helpful in understanding this spiritual impasse: "When they called for people to 'flee from the wrath to come,' Methodists did not generally have to convince people that God's wrath was coming."[13]

So that entrance exam to the Methodist Society was, in its day, a way of saying "all are welcome," because it spoke to the form that spiritual longing took in the religious culture of the time. By contrast, the religious imagination of our time, especially in large portions of Western society, simply doesn't include the images of eternal torment that have been the stock-in-trade of many a revival preacher. The promise of avoiding the wrath to come answers a question many people are not asking because they don't share the underlying sentiment.

Does that mean prevenient grace isn't at work anymore or isn't real? No, the Spirit reaches everyone. Whatever the Myers-Briggs Type Indicator[14] measures, it is clear God has created a variety of personality types. We learn and process information differently; so we experience the world, and the God who is in it finds us in our differences.

Here is another way to think of the fear that draws us to faith. As a child, I was afraid of Dracula and animals with sharp teeth. As an adult, I fear the death of a child, cancer, and the possibility of hitting someone while driving. But I think my true existential fear, and that of many others, isn't of a wrathful God or the consequences of our sins. Our worst fear is that there is no God. It's the nightmarish prospect that there is no meaning in the universe or in our lives. And the consequence at the end of mortal life isn't a hot orangish-red place out of Dante's *Inferno*. It's the cold, black empty nothingness of deep outer space.

Perhaps the most frightening movie villain in my lifetime is Hannibal Lector in *Silence of the Lambs*.[15] The chilling essence of his character isn't active malice; it's his emptiness of feeling. Indeed, the real-life horrors of our time are the random violence of terrorism and the mass murderers who stare out at us in news coverage with blank stares. The diseases of emptiness are the epidemics of drug abuse, depression, suicide, and (I think) the free-floating anger of our politics.

There is biblical warrant for this understanding of the experience of sin and death. The word *hell* may be translated as hollow or a dark cave. Matthew speaks of the torment of fire, but he also speaks of it as "the farthest darkness" (Matt 22:13 CEB). In Genesis, the time before creation is a world where "the earth was without shape or form, it was dark over the deep sea" (Gen 1:2 CEB). Indeed, sin has always been understood as the condition of being without God, with many of the psalms and the words of the prophets speaking about the torment of alienation from God.

# What Do You Hope For?

What, then, is God doing about it? What does it mean to be saved from this deep darkness? For Methodists, salvation isn't just a one-time transaction in the present for that time in the future when we enter God's kingdom. In his sermon "The Scripture Way of Salvation,"[16] John Wesley puts it this way: "It isn't something at a distance; it is a present thing; a blessing which, through the free mercy of God, ye are now in possession of." And in "The Way to the Kingdom," he uses the wonderfully evocative phrase: "Heaven opened in the soul." Read the following slowly and closely:

> This holiness and happiness, joined in one, are sometimes styled, in the inspired writings, "the kingdom of God" (as by our Lord in the text,) and sometimes "the kingdom of heaven." It is termed "the kingdom of God," because it's the immediate fruit of God's reigning in the soul. So soon as ever he takes unto himself his mighty power, and sets up his throne in our hearts, they

are instantly filled with this "righteousness, and peace, and joy in the Holy Ghost." It's called "the kingdom of heaven" because it is (in a degree) heaven opened in the soul. For whosoever they are that experience this, they can aver before angels and men.[17]

"Heaven opened in the soul" looms large in the Methodist religious imagination. Here's a way to understand it. Across Europe are magnificent Gothic cathedrals. If you can picture one in your mind, with all the spires and multiple roofs, perhaps you can imagine the effect on medieval people coming from miles away. They were the most significant buildings of their time, looming large on the landscape. And the architecture was meant to appear like a grand city from a distance. They were meant to inspire people who otherwise lived meagre and mundane lives to think of heaven and eternity. They were meant to be visual representations of Revelation 21:2: "I saw the Holy City, the New Jerusalem, coming down out of heaven from God" (CEB). Church buildings don't have that effect anymore. Now, the inner workings of the smartphone that takes a picture of the cathedral is just as impressive.

*American Methodists built cathedrals that were also meant to be witness to the kingdom come. Our cathedrals were the uncountable thousands of camp meetings and revivals of the nineteenth century, some among slaves unbeknownst to their owners. It was the congregations we established across the nation, the amazing foreign and domestic mission work of Methodist women, the Salvation Army, and Goodwill Industries. Our cathedrals are the countless orphanages, free clinics, settlement houses, hospitals, and colleges and universities that we instituted.*

47

These extraordinary works come from what Bill Shore of Share Our Strength calls "cathedrals within."[18] Methodists believe those originate with the Holy Spirit moving our hearts and minds over to God's way of thinking—literally "justifying" us, as the margin of this paragraph is justified to the sides of the page. The blueprint for these edifices come from heaven being opened in the soul, as described in Acts 2:17: "In the last days, God says, I will pour out my Spirit on all people. Your sons and daughters will prophesy. Your young will see visions. Your elders will dream dreams."

As people drove by my wife's church on 9/11, they saw the handwritten sign on the bedsheet announcing the service time. It didn't speak of sin or the "wrath to come," but it certainly reached the same depth of human need that night. And many of those who came in for the first time that night stayed in the congregation because they found a church with grace all sufficient to meet their fear and engage them in bright hope for the future.

## How Do We Maintain Discipline?

One feature of the current debate about LGBTQ people is the concern about flagrant violations of *The Book of Discipline of The United Methodist Church*. One argument against my proposal about what matters in Methodism is a legitimate and classically conservative argument. If what is essential is that we are experimenters in grace, isn't this reliance upon the Holy Spirit simply allowing anything and everything? Once you appear to have no rules, no fixed guidance, no agreed-upon standards, isn't the result chaos and the loss of any sense of a common identity?

As a matter of history, all the reformations of the church involve a loosening—or at least a reinterpretation, even a relaxation—of some aspects of received doctrine. But the critique is still valid. For instance, as I propose a local option about the acceptance of LGBTQ people, some people on both sides might ask, "How can you speak of accountable discipleship without some rule for holding one another accountable at either a congregational or denominational level?" But from my understanding of our essence as Methodists, I pose the following analogies in scripture. In Mark 10:17-27, when Jesus confronts the rich young man who is describing how he is following the letter of the law, doesn't Jesus convict him by questioning his inner, true commitment? And then in John 21:15, Jesus asks Peter three times, "Do you love me?" Isn't this a much harder question for Peter, a true test of his discipleship, than if Jesus asked, "Do you agree with me?"

*Chapter  3*

# CALL THE QUESTION

Davidd Field, in his book *Bid Our Jarring Conflicts Cease*, presents a compelling case for unity in The United Methodist Church based on John Wesley's own argument. Wesley envisioned the unity of the Methodist movement as a witness to the whole church through "its mission of forming a holy people whose presence and lives would bring reformation to the church and society."[1] Earlier, I suggested we are in a "delta region" in history. The delta includes both danger and potent opportunity. Can you imagine United Methodists emerging united from our present confusion and conflict? It truly would be a witness that we have found grace in a fractured time. And we would become a thirsty people able to tell other thirsty people where we found living water.

As I write this chapter, the Republicans in the United States Senate are trying to "repeal and replace" the 2010 Affordable Care Act. The Democrats favor "reform." In any event, substantial changes will be made in our health-care system, either by design or by default. So too, in the next few years, we will see a new United Methodist Church emerge because it's just not working anymore. This will happen either by thoughtful reform or by our inability to act.

To get there, we have some business to conduct as a denomination. I have never read Robert's Rules of Order all the way through. But I do know a motion to buy time: "I suggest the absence of a quorum." I also know the motion to end debate and get a vote: "Call the question!" It's time for us in The United Methodist Church to call the question, to move on from our understandable desire to gain unity, and to make some decisions. In order to thrive in the future, we need to take some decisive votes on bold proposals that can help us change and adapt. We don't have unanimity, but perhaps we have a quorum.

The issue immediately before us is our policy regarding LGBTQ people. As I proposed in the beginning of this book, I believe the best way forward on the questions of ordination and marriage ceremonies is an annual conference option. The annual conference is the fundamental unit of Methodism. *The Book of Discipline* is clear: clergy of the annual conference are those who decide all other issues of clergy selection and discipline. No doubt, this is a political compromise. So were the great ecumenical councils of the first millennium of the church, and this isn't one of those.

Even if we reach a resolution, and even if some churches leave, key questions remain about the nature and function of a global denomination. The following proposals focus on the role of the denominationas it affects the health of congregations in the US. What is the effect of the proposals I make on the central conferences (the collection of annual conferences outside the US)? That is beyond the scope of this book, but the questions should be: What is the effect on the central conferences if we are not able to stay united as Methodists? What is the effect if we can't address the decline of churches in the US?

# What Is the Role of the Denomination?

Archimedes said, "Give me a lever long enough and a fulcrum on which to place it, and I shall move the world." Or, as John Wesley said,

> Give me one hundred preachers who fear nothing but sin and desire nothing but God, and I care not a straw whether they be clergymen or laymen, such alone will shake the gates of hell and set up the kingdom of heaven upon earth.[2]

We have our mission as a denomination, but a key function of our connectionalism is to make wise and efficient use of our resources, which are our congregations and the clergy who flow from our seminaries. They are the fulcrum and the lever; this is where we should put our weight. Steve Lambert, former chair of the Wesley Seminary Board, has observed, referring to Paragraph 120 in the 2016 United Methodist *Book of Discipline*:

> Together we say we want to "Make disciples of Jesus Christ for the transformation of the world" and I think we mean it. We go on to announce that "Local churches and extension ministries of the Church provide the most significant arenas through which disciple-making occurs." If we believe what we say and want to be successful in achieving our mission, then our focus must not be diverted in any way from the local church and its ministries in the community. To do otherwise...to use our collective financial resources for purposes not directly helping the local church...is a formula for failure.[3]

How do we get to a level of clarity and agility at the denominational level to make wise use of resources? Ronald Heifetz and Marty Linsky, in *Leadership on the Line: Staying Alive through the Dangers of Leading,*[4] offer a helpful distinction between two kinds of leadership: technical and adaptive. Think of the difference between the mechanic, who can make a car work like it was designed; and an inventor, who designs a different vehicle. The technical leader is the leader of institutions; the adaptive leader is the leader of movements. We must be both. We aren't starting a movement, and most of us aren't planting a church. We are trying to reform an institution to get ourselves moving again.

Heifetz and Linsky suggest finding a "balcony" perspective. We have to be a part of the dance on the ballroom floor but also go up to the balcony to see the bigger picture below. Working for a seminary offers that opportunity. Here are three proposals from my vantage point: give time for a shared denominational vision to develop; act immediately to disrupt our recession; focus resources on congregations and clergy development.

## 1. Give Time for a Shared Denominational Vision to Develop

Here is my perspective about how to form institutional vision from the example of two of the eight General Conferences I have witnessed from the balcony. The first was Cleveland in 2000. Read the following excerpts from the story Bob Lear filed for the United Methodist News Service:

> The conference opened to the joyful beat of a band of bishops in the spectacular Rock and Roll Hall of Fame and Museum, and liturgical banners brightening the plenary hall in the Cleveland Convention Center.... Nine days later, that ornate hall became a confrontation zone with police placing 30 people, including two bishops, under arrest during a protest of the conference's vote retaining the church's controversial stance on homosexuality. It's believed to be the first time police that have been called to

remove demonstrators from a conference session. . . . Most of the particulars in the biggest single proposal for change—the much discussed Connectional Process Team (CPT) report—were overwhelmingly rejected.[5]

Even if you don't remember that particular conference, the report sounds depressingly familiar: a spectacular start, a conflict over LGBTQ people, and a failed attempt to reorganize. But I remember something else. It was a Friday morning when Millard Fuller, cofounder of Habitat for Humanity, made a powerful presentation. After listing the amazing results of Habitat nationwide, he said something like, "The greatest number of volunteers in our effort come from the United Methodists. Without them, Habitat could not have done this." You could feel the pride in the assembly.

Then Fuller spoke his vision that homelessness in America could be ended. As I was watching from the gallery, I was certain if someone figured out the right parliamentary trick, United Methodists would have taken on that task right there by acclamation. We would have figured out how to do it, and our future would have been quite different. Instead, we broke for lunch. And the spirit left the room. I mean that both metaphorically and mystically. When the conference took up the reorganization plan that had been developed diligently over four years by the Connectional Process Table, it failed.

It so happened that Millard Fuller appeared a year later as an example in an executive education program at the Harvard Business School (HBS) in which I prepared for my presidency. The focus of the program was how to scale up organizations. Habitat for Humanity was one of the case studies, and it featured Fuller's habit of casting visionary challenges. During the discussion, almost all the others in the group commented on how irresponsible he was. Most of the class participants thought this was a case study in bad leadership. The professor liked to provoke alternative views, and I was one of the few theologically trained in the group. So he asked me to explain what an "evangelist" is and what it means to be "prophetic." They imagined Habitat for Humanity should be run like a business and Fuller needed to get with the plan. They didn't know that in the beginning was the Word.

Fast forward to 2008 in Fort Worth. Richard Peck, then editor of *The Daily Christian Advocate*, wrote in his wrap-up report: "Earlier in the day, the delegates approved a $642 million denominational spending plan for the next four years built around four areas of focus for the immediate future."[6]

Some would say four goals are three too many. But there were ten initially, and four goals is remarkably resolute for such a diverse and sprawling body. The four goals had been selected through a complicated and lengthy set of steps that made use of a carefully designed and executed communication plan that included prepared speeches, talking points, and video packets. Each goal represented ideas that had been developed from the bottom up. The process would make an excellent business school case study.

Because time was allotted to develop the goals, the spending plan passed in an anxious year with strong support and real enthusiasm. In fact, the 2008 goals, structuring our work at various levels in the denomination, motivated congregational and annual conference giving. For instance, the very successful "Imagine No Malaria" campaign came out of this process.

*We must get to that point where annual conference and general conference sessions become the culmination of a broad and deeply shared vision coming from congregations who are experiencing new life from a new sense of their mission. But we are not there yet. This will have to come later. First we have to do the work to foster a shared vision.*

### Foster a Shared Vision

Taken together, the events of the two conferences show the importance of fostering a shared vision, which is the central task of adaptive leadership. The first case, in 2000, failed because delegates were presented with a complex, comprehensive plan for restructuring without a compelling vision. Fuller's vision hung out there like Jeremiah's prophecy. We were not prepared to hear it, and a plan was already on the floor.

A shared vision is more than an organizational plan and a denominational slogan. And, while vision must include what *Good to Great* author Jim Collins calls "Big Hairy Audacious Goals,"[7] leaders simply dreaming up and drafting those "BHAGs" isn't sufficient. The big goals in 2008 were owned by the connection before they were proposed, and the vision was compelling.

*A new church will come from a shared vision that expresses what we are going to do together and how we are going to be engaged in our mission. But how we get to that vision is crucial. The shared vision has to come from both the deep yearnings and the best selves of those who must ultimately support it.*

Developing a vision that calls forth the better angels of our nature is the necessary skill of political leadership. Some of our reorganization plans and many annual conference capital campaigns have failed in recent years because we as leaders have lost this almost instinctive touch with the base. This is like a problem our two national political parties have at this writing.

Losing touch with the base is an occupational hazard, particularly for clergy. We are enculturated to think our job is to talk. We assume we are the vision casters, the explainers. But I've also come to realize that, in a time such as this, leadership requires more vision *gathering* than vision *casting.*

Today we should be trying to give voice to a collective sense of the movement of the Holy Spirit. For example, I've watched some of the best preachers in historically black denominations preach in the call and response tradition. They follow the first rule of a trial lawyer in front of a witness. They don't ask a question they don't already know the answer to. So when they ask "Can I get an amen?" they get it because they have worked hard for it beforehand. Betty Beene, former CEO of United Way of America, captured the essence of this practice as she tutored me in leadership. She gave me the most helpful advice I have ever received: "People support what they help to create."

## 2. Act Immediately to Disrupt Our Recession

Simultaneously, we have to deal with our economic challenge. Our recession is in membership, attendance, and general vitality, but understanding economic recessions is instructive. In this I am indebted to my mentor and former board chair, the late Edward W. Kelley from St. Luke's United Methodist Church in Houston. As a Reagan appointee to the Federal Reserve Board, he tutored me in economics and guided my presidency.

In a consumer-driven economy, the natural tendency is to save money and slow down spending, but this has the perverse effect of deepening a recession. This is why President Bush asked us to shop after 9/11 and the Federal Reserve pumped money into the economy to avert a total collapse in 2008–2009.

Unlike a nation, The United Methodist Church can't print money. So where will the funds come from? In a recession, the nation diverts funds to activities that build capacity for future growth. If we apply that principle to the denomination, it means now is the time to save funds in some areas and make investments in others at a level of magnitude that gives us a chance of breaking the recessionary cycle by investing in those activities that will bring a spiritual renewal and organizational vitality.

One possibility for such a redirection of investment exists because funds don't flow smoothly or immediately between levels of the denomination. Instead, apportionments are at times diverted into pools of reserve funds in some of our general church agencies where they often sit and grow with investments. They also can collect in annual conferences, where some past MEF money and other funds collected and received in previous years now sit. Now is the time to release these funds for growth. This is the rainy day.

But those funds aren't enough. We must reduce spending not associated with congregational vitality immediately. Lovett Weems addresses this in his book *Focus*. He describes the "necessity of a fundamental resetting of the financial baseline at all levels of the church."[8] All his proposals are still valid, and the book merits a rereading. Generally, Weems calls for strict, outcomes-based evaluation of the role, size, and programs of the church at all levels rather than simply setting percentage increases or decreases.

The Lewis Center has focused its attention on the dismal demographics of the denomination. Inevitably, we will continue to see a decline in membership over the next fifteen years. To some extent, this will reduce expenses to the degree general church apportionments are tied to net expenditures of local churches. Some think it could happen in a gradual, soft landing.

*I believe there is a very strong possibility of precipitous—not gradual—decline in revenue. This can happen in one or more ways: if a significant number of congregations leave in schism; if larger and growing churches begin refusing to bear an increasing burden of apportionments; or if there is another national economic recession. If it's not already too late, we should ease off the gas now rather than slam on the brakes later.*

Weems's suggested reductions in 2012 included substantially reducing the cost of the General Conference and annual conference sessions themselves and reducing and consolidating the work of the boards and agencies. This intervention nearly happened in 2012 through the Call to Action, but special interests in the three branches of UMC polity (executive, legislative, and judicial) were unable to agree and ratify the legislation. Meanwhile, one easy part of the solution in the age of sophisticated communications technology is to go paperless. Another is to take a hard look at travel costs. Much is spent to create the appearance and experience of a global church for a very small number of people.

General agency apportionments have gone down significantly as a percentage of total church giving. The staff of our judicatories are good people who work hard. They did not create this problem. But it's time to recognize that neither General Church agencies and General Conference initiatives nor Annual Conference program staff significantly affect membership, attendance, and giving in the local church, which is where the recession can be reversed. Moreover, a significant reduction in expenses by the denomination's structure would have a strong symbolic and political effect. It sends an important signal that we mean to do business differently.

However, the only way to make a significant difference is to reduce our biggest long-term liability: the cost of clergy. This will require even more decisive action.

### *Restructure Our Assets and Liabilities*

We should look at our biggest asset and our biggest liability together. Our biggest asset is our underutilized church property. If we were a company, we would be ripe for a hostile takeover. We have far too many churches in the wrong places due to denominational mergers, demographic shifts, and an unwillingness to make hard decisions relating to closures of local churches.

Our biggest liability is what I would call our "clergy legacy cost," similar to the legacy cost faced by the big auto manufacturers. We have ordained far too many elders over the last sixty years. They have lived longer than expected, experiencing ever-rising health-care costs. Moreover, too many congregations are not able to support the full weight of salary and benefits of the full-time clergy appointed to them.

Many believe ending guaranteed appointment is a necessary part of the equation. I have a somewhat different view. The main reason for our current problem isn't that we have an unusual number of incompetent pastors. We simply have too high a clergy legacy cost. This is on us as leaders. And, to the extent some of our pastors are ineffective, that is on us too. Instead, we should, henceforth, limit certification for ordained ministry only to those who show high promise for effectiveness and ordain only as many as we expect to be able to support. And, in those instances of ineffective pastors who can't or won't change, we must simply have the courage to remove.

I recognize the disposition of capital assets and the cost of clergy are normally annual conference responsibilities. But I believe we need to see these issues as a national problem because, just as a rising tide lifts all boats, an ebbing tide lowers all boats—and a tsunami sinks all boats.

*We need a forum to develop both practical proposals and the courage to face these two issues: the clergy legacy cost and the underutilized capital resources.*

Such a forum could achieve consequential results, like the National Commission on Social Security Reform that produced the Social Security Reform Act of 1983, avoiding insolvency for a generation, and the Base Realignment and Closing process that closed 350 military installations. These were successful bipartisan, blue-ribbon efforts to both accelerate and bypass normal political processes. A denominational forum could produce a template, a national plan, for annual conferences to consider and implement.

## 3. Focus Resources on Congregations and Clergy Development

*Simply reducing expenses, however, will not end the recession in our vitality. We must also fund activities that foster recovery. We need to invest in the local church and its missions and ministry. We should divert resources to the congregations that show the most promise for future growth and allow them to experiment to see where the Spirit's moving us into new fields of mission. And we should invest in preparing the next generation of clergy to be innovative leaders of congregations, where disciples of Jesus Christ are made.*

### *Focus on Congregations*

Our failure to close redundant local churches, and the excess elders in congregations that can't afford them, means we forgo many opportunities for new church starts. Meanwhile, we rely on the growing and stronger congregations to fund the clergy legacy costs as part of their annual conference apportionment. Those same congregations are also bearing most of the cost of new buildings. This means we reduce the missional potential of those vital churches and our conferences as a whole. It's as if we have gone through the vineyard and pruned the very vines that are producing fruit.

If we are going to reverse our denominational recession in vitality, we must invest now in those local congregations and regions that are demonstrating fruitfulness. From this action now will be a harvest for all of us later because of a new potential for a shared vision.

In the next chapter, I suggest some ways to think about how congregations can seek this revitalization. Here, I describe how we must focus resources on our clergy.

### *Care for Our Clergy*

*It's a pity and a shame to speak of clergy as "liabilities" because at a deeper level they are our most precious asset. They are our leaders and often are the very embodiment of our mission in the world. They are disciples of Christ answering God's call to a life of service. What I am proposing is to deal with the legacy cost of too many clergy while simultaneously investing in future leaders.*

Franklin Gillis, a leading pastor in my annual conference, used to greet another clergyperson with: "How is it with your soul?"

That immediately shaped the ensuing conversation, drawing the circle of vocation around the conversation. It's not surprising that he was a mentor to many pastors and was the reason a number of people pursued ordained ministry. The business management guru Peter Drucker is often quoted saying, "You can only manage what you measure." What if we could measure the level of "how is it with your soul" conversations among the clergy? I believe that would be the way to truly end the spiritual recession among Methodists, creating a virtuous cycle of grace and holiness.

Wesley Seminary is a lead partner in a major multiyear, multi-denominational study of how clergy can remain resilient and effective over the long term. The study, entitled "The Flourishing in Ministry Project," is being conducted by Matt Bloom of the Mendoza College of Business at Notre Dame University.[9] Matt, his clergy partner Kim Bloom, and their team have conducted surveys and in-depth interviews of thousands of clergy. Now we are working together to find ways to translate this research to systems of clergy formation.

The most exciting aspect of this research is that it is not focused on the pathologies of ministry. Rather, this work helps reveal how clergy can remain emotionally healthy. As they say, "Flourishing happens when ministry is a life-enriching rather than life-depleting experience."[10]

Matt and Kim describe what seminaries ought to be doing to help their students prepare to flourish in ministry. The key is to help them form their pastoral identity. That begins with discovering who they are at a deep level and how they will be integrated with what is expected of pastoral ministry. If this happens the pastor can develop deep and authentic relationships with people as pastors and cultivate "How is it with your soul?" relationships with other pastors in a shared understanding of the joys and challenges of ministry, along with a shared vision of the transcendent purpose of their work.

In theory, for most denominations, including United Methodists, this formation includes the process of ordination. However, the time in seminary is, by far, the extensive and intensive opportunity for this to happen. And, in theory, the two processes—seminary and ordination—should be in close conversation and mostly parallel. But, in fact, the denominational process is perceived by most students as a job interview, and seminary is usually experienced as a race (the root meaning of the word *curriculum*).

Moreover, research shows the early years of ministry after seminary and ordination are critical periods for the development of pastoral identity.

For more than a decade, beginning in 2002, the Lilly Endowment funded an initiative called "Sustaining Pastoral Excellence," focused on providing peer support and learning for clergy, including younger clergy. Penny Long Marler's book *So Much Better: How Thousands of Pastors Help Each Other Thrive* reports on some of the key practices by which clergy can support one another as peers:

> Pastoral peers 1. Gather around their calling; 2. Make an intentional covenant for spiritual support, theological challenge, and mutual accountability; 3. Spend time with one another in prayer, at meals, and through travel; and 4. Take what (and how) they've learned into their ministries. In doing so, they replicate a first-century disciple model. This kind of peer learning is sacred practice.[11]

This describes the dynamic behind clergy thriving and flourishing. Two findings in the Flourishing in Ministry study are important to note. One is how much a pastor's identity is determined by the relationship with the congregation; however, a large number of clergy in the study report that members of their congregations never ask them, "How are you doing?" The second finding is while denominational officials rank second after the congregation (and ahead of clergy families) as influencers of clergy well-being, the influence is more likely to be negative. The research shows bishops, district superintendents, and boards of ordained ministry are more likely to diminish than enhance the well-being of clergy.

These findings should be of special interest to United Methodists because, in theory, as United Methodist clergy we don't belong to the congregation we serve: we belong to each other in our annual conference. But the Flourishing in Ministry research shows no difference between United Methodists and other denominations. Caring for each other's souls as clergy is another part of the genetic inheritance I described. We are to be for each other means of sanctifying grace.

A central feature of a new church and a new seminary will be a joint effort to create the conditions for clergy to flourish, especially from the time they enter seminary through their early years in ministry. This will require annual conferences and seminaries to work together to explore new patterns of coordinating our processes and make them seem less like "process" and more like true "holy conferencing."

An essential part of caring for clergy is to care for their financial well-being, which is jeopardized by the debt they incur in college and seminary. Several of the United Methodist seminaries are part of a multiyear study funded by Lilly Endowment to develop ways to reduce clergy indebtedness. The schools in the study have already helped their students reduce their borrowing through courses and coaching in financial literacy and personal financial management.[12] However, frugality is only part of the solution in an era when 20 percent or less of the cost of seminary education is covered by the church, which once supported over 80 percent of the cost.

*We should have as our goal debt-free seminary education for United Methodists in our United Methodist seminaries through a combination of seminary-funded scholarships, congregational support, and denominational loans that would be forgiven in exchange for years of service.* ✓

We should also not overlook the increasing number of bi-vocational clergy. Many already serving are those we refer to as "local pastors." They serve in small rural churches, either part-time or full-time. But in the future, many of the new part-time pastors will be young and urban or suburban. This is because some of the best candidates in seminary today believe they can't afford to be in ministry full-time given the decline of the church and the shrinking number of full-time appointments. But they are called to ministry and willing to serve.

We must work together to find ways to better form these men and women in their pastoral identity, which includes their financial health as well.

In the conferences, we must look without flinching at the balance of full-time and part-time clergy—and guaranteed minimum salary. In the past, this has been thought of as a theological question about the meaning of ordination. But we've studied ministry for over twenty years and haven't figured that out. We must focus instead on this as a practical and measurable problem. As Lovett Weems said recently: "We have two policies that are moving toward a potential crisis—guaranteed appointment and minimum salary."

## Too Many Seminaries?

I realize in a time of seeming scarcity and declining resources, I am advocating increased spending on new clergy. Moreover, I urge us to maintain the current dollar level of MEF support adjusted for inflation. So it's fair to ask again the question I posed at the beginning: Do we have too many seminaries? Yes, I think we do. How can that number be reduced? There is no central authority. We are the seminaries of the denomination, but we are also independently governed either by self-perpetuating boards or embedded in major universities. There is no United Methodist entity that can close a seminary by fiat.

Of course, a way to accomplish this goal is to continue to cut MEF funding. But that weakens everyone. And it may be the case that some of the seminaries most dependent on MEF funding are schools we need for missional reasons. The heads of our schools would be quick to join me in pointing out that each of us has an ethical responsibility to care for our own schools. Also, our seminaries serve other denominations and the world, as well as The UMC. Indeed, we believe that outreach is part of our mission as United Methodists.

Nevertheless, the CEOs of the thirteen United Methodist theological seminaries have agreed to come together as colleagues with members of our boards or representatives from host universities, to develop proposals to address the general issue of denominational recession. We are already meeting with key denominational leaders and the pastors of substantial churches to consider ways to contain student costs and reduce student debt. This work could build on the study already commissioned by the thirteen seminaries to study the viability and sustainability of a system of thirteen seminaries within The UMC, along with the almost forty additional non-UMC schools approved for the education of those who seek ordination. The study should be complete by the end of 2018.

# Pruning to Flourish

*The business of the church isn't business. Jesus said the faith community is like a grapevine: "I am the vine, you are the branches" (John 15:5 CEB). The vinedresser prunes the vine so that it might flourish, so that the world might flourish. This chapter proposed ways in which we can focus the attention and resources of the denomination on that part of the vine that bears fruit—on effective schools, congregations, and clergy leadership—that they may focus on the business of being worthy agents of the kingdom of God. From this work comes the new energy to foster a shared vision of mission and ministry for The United Methodist Church for the sake of the world.*

*Chapter 4*

# DISRUPTIVE
# INNOVATION

**Millennials, Message, and Missional Churches**

I n the preceding chapter, I recommend that this is the time to focus our resources on local churches and the development of clergy leadership as our path to a new church and a new seminary. But what can they do to break the cycle of decline? A line in the movie *The Blues Brothers* is my private mantra. Jake and Elwood (played by Jim Belushi and Dan Aykroyd), wearing black suits, black fedoras, and dark glasses, announce, "We're on a mission from God" (pronounced "Ghad" in their Chicago accent). In the movie, the brothers disrupt the police, families, church services, and traffic from Chicago to Calumet City. People on a mission will be disruptive.

## Disruptive Innovation

"Disruptive innovation" is a helpful way to think about changing institutions. It's a phrase coined by Clayton Christensen from the Harvard Business School.[1] The research question he explores is: Why do strong, seemingly well-led companies fail to take advantage of new possibilities that are right under their noses? Why did Sears with its catalog fail to become Walmart, then Amazon?

Christensen concluded it's not because of bad leadership. Instead, it's *because* those organizations were successful. They had a popular brand, well-honed business practices, and a web of customers and suppliers. All of this works really well, then OK, then not as good as it used to. But at no point do the alternatives seem able to replace what they have. Doesn't this describe The United Methodist Church and its seminaries over the last forty years?

Finding and incorporating promising disruptive innovations is how we can become a new seminary and a new church. Christensen admits, this is rare for any established organization to accomplish. It requires a period of incubation, like "urban enterprise zones," where new businesses are given relief from taxes and regulations to find their sustainable business model by trial and error.

One example might be like that of several congregations in my region designed to reach the poor. They are not expected to pay full apportionments, and they receive support in the form of money and volunteers. These are worthy efforts, but it's interesting to note these churches are often called "missions" in a way that seems to relegate them to the periphery. If they are mission churches, what are the other churches?

However, a distinctive characteristic of a true innovative disruption is that it will ultimately change the system in which it's incubated. In a literal sense, seminaries are supposed to be incubators, since the very word *seminary* is Latin for seed plot.

We usually think of students as the seed, but we also have other things growing within our walls. Think of the nineteenth-century monk Gregor Mendel whose experiments with pea plants in the monastery gardens made him the father of modern genetics; or think of the way monasteries, as centers of learning, protected ancient manuscripts during the Dark Ages. Two core purposes of academic communities are to develop new ideas and to protect old ones until their time has come again.

*Seminaries are where new ideas and practices are incubated. Even though they seem impractical now, some may be the key to the future. In fact, seminaries should be innovative disrupters precisely because we are the conservers of the idealism of the Christian community.*

What are the disruptive innovations we should be thinking about? Among the current candidates are online technology, non-degree professional education, and lay education. These fit the criteria: they are emerging, they are not part of the traditional "business" of graduate theological education, and they are not now profitable. These may be part of the answer, but let's explore more fundamental disruptions.

I met with Christensen as I thought about this chapter. We share a common interest because he is a leader in the Mormon Church and was interested in talking with me about how his research could help both of our traditions. The Mormons are a very interesting study for Methodists.[2] We view the Latter-Day Saints as a strong movement. However, they have stopped growing in the US and would be declining were it not for a high birthrate. Their only growth is overseas.

# Millennials as the Disruptive Innovation

So Christensen and I discussed how the concept of disruptive innovation might create opportunities for our churches. We focused on the millennial generation because the Mormons are having as difficult a time as the rest of us in cracking that generational code. As churches of all denominations struggle to turn around their aging congregations, there is a lot of hope invested in attracting those born between 1982 and 2002. To some young visitors, an encounter with an old congregation may seem like an ecclesiastical zombie movie—the walking dead grasping for the living in order to survive. If I were a member of that generation, I'd run screaming.

Wesley Seminary has embarked on a major Lilly Endowment–funded research project to learn from those faith communities who are figuring out how to attract and incorporate young adults. Together, teams from these congregations are forming an Innovation Hub, through which we will explore not just what attracts millennials but what we can build with millennials. We will be looking at this research with a different angle. Because, in a very short period of time, this generation will be the largest segment of clergy.

*Instead of asking: "How can we attract millennials?" we will be asking "What kind of church will millennials lead?"*

Here are some things we already know that show millennials would make good Methodists.

## *1. Millennials Are Searching for a Deep and Authentic Faith*

Kenda Creasy Dean is one of the leading researchers in youth and young adult ministry. In her book *Almost Christian*, she reflects on the National Study of Youth and Religion conducted by the Pew Research Center. She draws some sobering conclusions about youth and young adults in mainline Protestant churches and why we lose them. "We've successfully convinced teenagers that religious participation is important for moral formation and for making nice people. What we have been less able to convey to young people is faith."[3]

The current form and practices of the institutional church are not working. It can't be assumed that the faith Kenda talks about will come in the way it might have for previous generations. Like the second-generation Korean-American students in our seminary, the millennials honor the faith of their fathers and mothers but are looking for a faith that speaks to their hearts. This desire is reminiscent of what gave rise to Methodism in the first place. John Wesley was looking for *real* Christianity and how to become *altogether a Christian*, not just *almost a Christian*.[4]

## *2. Millennials Want to Save the World, Not the Church*

The stereotype of this generation is legions of young college graduates who want to work for nonprofits or international nongovernmental organizations. I've seen many come to Washington, DC.

But like all generations, millennials are not all the same. Many enter the military and intelligence agencies with a post-9/11 desire to serve. Millennials are less liberal/progressive than the previous two generations at their same age.[5] Yet some are the energy behind the new civil rights movements, such as Black Lives Matter. Many are the Dreamers, the children of undocumented immigrants. This is the generation of LGBTQ who will not stay in the closet.

Millennials are the first generation since World War II who experienced a prolonged period of joblessness. They want to see change yet don't trust established institutions to deliver. That includes the church. But my generation should recognize this suspicion as consistent with a very Methodist characteristic, because we were a movement born in mission. We were reluctant, at first, to even think of ourselves as a church.

## 3. Millennials Have Moved Beyond the Faith versus Works Debate

The great debate that produced Protestantism was over the question of what is necessary for salvation. Martin Luther took his stand on *sola fide*, "faith alone." There is a distorted modern version of this that we hear from many people among my generation and older: "I come to church to be fed spiritually. I don't want to hear about social issues from the pulpit. It's fine for the church to do good work, but there are nonprofits that do that kind of thing. The focus of the church should be on building up faith."

By contrast, millennials don't differentiate between building faith and doing good work. Similarly, Methodists have always believed the Christian faith, even salvation itself, isn't a choice between the two. Not only are good works required of the faithful, they are also, through the Holy Spirit, a source of sanctifying grace.[6]

"The church is always just one generation from extinction." This statement is so ubiquitous in Christianity the original source can't be determined. This scripture passage probably is its foundation: "*When that whole generation had passed away, another generation came after them who didn't know the Lord or the things that he had done for Israel*" (Judg 2:10).

*The millennial generation is a disruptive innovation that has some behaviors consistent with the traditions of Methodism. The challenge for the last act of the retiring baby boomer generation of seminary and church leaders is determining how to enable and empower this generation to disrupt us.*

# Our Message as the Disruptive Innovation

At the same time, as millennials rise to leadership they should consider that Christianity has within itself the capacity for its own renewal. Every new movement in Christianity grew as a new shoot on the old vine: from Saint Francis to Luther and Wesley; from the secret worship services of slaves to the church communities in Latin America who lead resistance movements to the cell churches in China. All have drawn from the inherently subversive message of the gospel.

*Our message, the good news of Jesus Christ, is an eternally disruptive innovation. As Paul said to the new church in Corinth, who were already forgetting who they were:*

*But we preach Christ crucified, which is a scandal to Jews and foolishness to Gentiles. But to those who are called—both Jews and Greeks—Christ is God's power and God's wisdom. This is because the foolishness of God is wiser than human wisdom, and the weakness of God is stronger than human strength. (1 Cor 1:23-25 CEB)*

# Mission as Disruptive Innovation

The challenge and frustration of Christian leaders since Paul is that simply preaching disruptive wisdom from the pulpit and demonstrating it at the Communion table is necessary but not sufficient for continually renewing the church from generation to generation and fulfilling the Great Commandment and the Great Commission.

As we continually struggle in United Methodism to redesign our understanding of ordination, we still come back to Word, sacrament, and order to describe the key roles for leadership in the Christian community.

*Ordering our congregational lives as an alternative called and sent community can allow the Holy Spirit to disrupt our lives and the life of our church and to make us, as members of the Body of Christ, a disruptive innovation for the rest of the church and for the world.*

Some say that George Whitfield was a better preacher in his day than John Wesley and drew bigger crowds, especially in America. But no church survived after the echo of Whitfield's preaching died, while Wesley's genius was his organizational ability. Those of us charged with the ordering of The United Methodist Church and the leadership of our seminaries are trying to make something new out of something old without losing what is essential or destroying congregations and structures that are doing good in the world and are still meaningful for the seven million people who still think of themselves as members of this denomination in the US.

In the practice of this kind of leadership, we have to have objectivity about the real world and make tough choices that often affect the lives of people. But we are also subjects of a new world that should look very different from the old. I often think of Jesus's advice: "I'm sending you as sheep among wolves. Therefore, be wise as snakes and innocent as doves" (Matt 10:16 CEB).

# The Missional Church

In the late 1990s, the phrase *missional church* became well known in the US, due at first to the work of theologian and missiologist Lesslie Newbigin. After retiring in 1974 from missionary work in India, Newbigin found a second mission field: modern Western culture.[7] His fundamental concept has been picked up by many thought leaders and church renewal movements. One is Alan Hirsch, who helpfully contrasts *missional* evangelism with *attractional* evangelism (recall my description of mule churches as member-service organizations). He is also one of many who speak of this as *apostolic* ministry in an attempt to reboot to the early days of Christianity.[8]

By its simple definition, it's hard to see how the concept of the missional church is disruptive. It seems like one of those exercises you go through at the beginning of a church planning retreat. On the first couple of sheets of newsprint, the church's mission is remembered or reformulated. The result is an affirmation something like this: "Our mission is to be involved in God's mission in the world; our organizing principle is to share the good news about Jesus Christ, which is the kingdom of God." A similar exercise created The United Methodist mission statement: "The mission of the Church is to make disciples of Jesus Christ for the transformation of the world."[9] The gap between a perfected statement of mission and actual practice is wide.

*An important emphasis of this movement is to insist on the difference between* missions *as discrete programs of the church and* missional *as a fundamental identity of the church. It's the difference between thinking of* mission *as the projects a church conducts once it's strong and has enough discretionary time and money, versus* mission *as the very source of congregational vitality.*

However, to be a missional church finally depends on what we do, not who we say when we are on retreat. When the Blues Brothers said they were "on a mission from God," the "mission" was to "get the band back together." It has to do with what our budgets and our calendars demonstrate we actually do. This is how we change from being a member-services church to a missional church. Some will push back, asking, "Isn't serving members part of our mission?" Not if we understand that God is calling everyone to ministry. We are, each individually and all together, missional people. And we should be asking ourselves if we are answering our God's call in our time and place.

Bill Gibb is a retired lawyer and longtime member of a United Methodist church in the Maryland suburbs. He read drafts of this book and asked questions. When he read this chapter, he sent back this question: "You stress the importance of becoming missional as compared to carrying out discrete mission programs. I am unclear as to what this means for my church that has a significant number of mission programs; does it need to do more? How do you know when it becomes 'missional'?" Good question. There is no definitive test, and every pastor I know is trying hard. We have always recognized the importance of membership by "professions of faith." What are some additional measurements? Some objective clues might be whether the church budgeting process takes risks on behalf of those Jesus said we should. And whether the church is producing fruit in growth of souls who think of that church as home. But equally important is whether the congregation senses itself to be growing in grace. When I was a musician, there were times when our band found our groove, and we knew it while we were playing. In a church, it's the experience that God is calling us all, and we're hearing it and trying to answer it. It's the experience of sanctifying grace.

In my experience while leading many church retreats, some will embrace change and some will not. The difference, the x-factor in the equation, is a shared vision as I described in the previous chapter. And this comes from a long process of cultivating wisdom and courage as virtues of the congregation.

The African American church is one of the great stories of being a missional church in the history of world Christianity. It provided solace and subversive support for slaves and their oppressed descendants. It facilitated the Great Migration of African Americans from the rural south to the urban north. And it fed and led the Civil Rights Movement.

And yet, even for these historic African American congregations, disruptive innovation is necessary today. Doug Powe describes the new challenge in his book *New Wine, New Wineskins: How African American Congregations Can Reach New Generations:* "It's time for many African American congregations to recognize it isn't enough to simply be the church. It's time to rethink the meaning of church for those who came after the civil rights struggle."[10]

United Methodists should be perfectly suited to foster missional disruptive innovation, because our genetic legacy is to be "experimenters in grace," as I described earlier. And so, as we consider how to redistribute resources to congregations, we should be funding the experiments that focus on our mission and stay on the message of salvation, realizing the experiments will fail at the same rate as new businesses (about 50 percent fail before the fifth year). One of the exciting ventures in this direction is the organization Ministry Incubators, founded by Kenda Creasy Dean. She says, "Our goal is to help people turned hare-brained ideas into sustainable ministries."[11]

Rosabeth Moss Kanter, at the Harvard Business School, suggests a helpful image for experimenting in what I have called the "delta region." She says we should think of ourselves as being in "improvisational theater." There is a stage, a plot, and actors, but they are given the flexibility to interact and improvise.

*What if we think of the new church and the new seminary as improvisational theater? In our play, the Holy Spirit is the protagonist (or sometimes the antagonist) as we seek to get the band back together, on a mission from God?*

*Chapter 5*

# SEMINARIES ARE THE SOLUTION, PART 1

## A Community of Wisdom and Courage

The subtitle of this book suggests seminaries are the solution to the formation of a new church. Really? Sometimes, I get mail addressed to Wesley Theological Cemetery. Can a place dedicated to preserving tradition also be the driver of innovation? Can seminaries be self-differentiated servant leaders in this delta region of the early twenty-first century? I suggested in the previous chapter that we *are* the disruptive innovators for the church and that the church itself—its message and its mission—is the disruptive innovator in the world.

*What's missing in our world is a critical mass of informed missional people willing to make sacrifices after the example of Christ. I'm reminded of the words of Jesus: "You are the salt of the earth. But if salt loses its saltiness, how will it become salty again? It's good for nothing except to be thrown away and trampled under people's feet" (Matt 5:13 CEB). Truly, if we are not part of the solution, we are part of the problem. We need a new church to meet the challenges of this age. For this, we need a new seminary.*

# Traditioned Innovation

The secret to faithful and adaptive leadership is in the relationship between tradition and innovation. Thinking of a sailboat on that delta, it isn't the difference between the anchor and the sail. Greg Jones, former dean of Duke Divinity School, coined the phrase "traditioned innovation" to describe the way we should think of being entrepreneurial as Christians.[1] Tradition, the things we teach in seminary (scripture, history, theology, and rituals), is the raw material for innovation. Perhaps it's helpful to think of our tradition as the sailcloth. And then we are not inventors; we are discoverers. Our task is to set our sails artfully and correctly to catch the winds of the Holy Spirit.

Just as the denomination and local congregations must think about how to navigate these waters, we must do the same as seminaries. And so I divided my vision for how "seminaries are the solution" into two parts. In this chapter, I describe how we, at our best, are a community providing the essential elements of traditional ministerial practice. In the next chapter, I suggest how we need to innovative and become something new to extend the resources of our seminaries beyond the graduate school model.

# The Intellectual and Moral Challenge

Here is some background for another thought experiment. While I was writing this chapter early one Sunday morning, I was watching the Charlie Rose show. He was interviewing scientists who were explaining the latest breakthrough in genetic engineering. They had successfully altered an abnormal gene in an embryo, thus eliminating a disease from that family line. When this process is perfected, it will cure many diseases. But it could also further separate the haves from the have-nots—genetically as well as financially.

Think of other potential developments with ethical implications. Soon human cloning will be perfected. A computer will seem to acquire consciousness. Life may be discovered on other planets. Global warming and resource inequality will raise fundamental questions of viability and fairness. Psychologists may claim to predict the future criminal record of newborns, and sociologists the voting patterns of adults, as the economic and behavioral sciences become more manipulative and deterministic. I suspect there were very few sermons in the last year about any of these issues that raise fundamental questions about the value of a person and the meaning of human life.

One seminary dean once worried about the "dumbing down of the clergy." I know that is harsh, but just as America is falling behind in the global economy because not enough of our children are excelling in science, technology, engineering, and math, American Christianity is becoming marginalized because it's increasingly ill-equipped to explore the theological dimension of the great scientific, social, political, and psychological issues of the day.

Meanwhile, it's a time of great opportunity to *do good* well. Advances in science, technology, finance, communications, and management make it possible to cure disease, bring peace among nations, be good stewards of the planet, send relief and resources anywhere on earth, cool the planet, and end extreme poverty.

And this is an age of strong spiritual yearning combined with weakening religious traditions. Pastors are called to minister in a society more religiously diverse, perhaps, than any since the Greco-Roman world of the first-century church. Like then, we encounter people we call *unchurched,* as though they just haven't found the one they like. In fact, the local mission field is now full of people who know nothing about what we have to offer, in addition to those who once went to church and people of other faith traditions.

Meanwhile, many American Christians are caught in a downward spiral of irrelevancy as a defensive, willful ignorance about science is treated as if ignorance is a virtue, and religion becomes a retreat from the complexity of society. Simultaneously, the symptoms of an anxious society have caused clergy to become more *pastoral* in the sense of being protective and providing emotional comfort. But this shift has also made us more timid, draining the word *pastor* of its essential meaning, which is leader.

So, here is the thought experiment: given the intellectual and moral challenges of our time, do we think we require fewer well-educated pastors? Do we think cost and convenience should determine whether someone goes to seminary?

*What does traditional seminary education have to offer? I invite you to think about it as I did one Sunday during the opening hymn. Focus on this one stanza of "God of Grace and God of Glory": "Grant us wisdom, grant us courage, for the living of these days."[2] More than the transfer of information, these two virtues—wisdom and courage—are still the two most important things acquired through time-intensive, face-to-face theological education.*

# Grant Us Wisdom

The best description I have for the work of a seminary teacher comes from Supreme Court Justice Oliver Wendell Holmes's description of the search for truth. He wrote, "I would not give a fig for the simplicity this side of complexity, but I would give my life for the simplicity on the other side of complexity."[3]

How do you arrive at the simplicity on the other side of complexity? In a very limited amount of time, what do you teach a future leader of the Christian faith? For example, think about how you would answer this series of deceptively simple questions:

- Who was Jesus?

- Why did Jesus die?

- Did Jesus *really* die?

- Why does this matter today?

You can appreciate the challenge if you've ever tried to help a middle-schooler with algebra and found yourself at that point of utter frustration when he says, "Dad, just tell me the answer!" Seminary education isn't just a matter of accumulating knowledge, it's a way of thinking. It's the building of wisdom.

How do faculty approach this challenge? At one end of the pedagogical spectrum is rote memorization of names and facts and doctrines. At the other end is value-neutral training in critical thinking skills. Faculty take a third approach. They build a kind of trellis with staves of history and biblical scholarship and lathes of theological reflection so that new knowledge and insight can climb like a vine. Educators call this craft *scaffolding*. The process of building and developing a faculty is also scaffolding to produce a school of thought. Like the vinedresser in John 15:1, teachers and deans make choices so that the vine will be fruitful. This educational process among faculty and students is how wisdom is formed.

Prior to the 2016 General Conference of The United Methodist Church, the United Methodist seminary CEOs were asked to develop a statement about the role of our seminaries. Rather than produce a defense of our institutions in the hope of protecting the MEF, we produced the document found in the appendix: "The Value of Scholarship for Theological Education," which reflects who we all are at our core.

*The saying goes, "Seeing is believing. But believing is also a way of seeing." Theology is like optometry or audiology, forming habits of the mind and heart to see or hear God's presence. Students come to seminary with a faith formed in a particular circumstance. Sometimes they come with a false sense of pride that what they know must be all they need to know. But then they enter the academy, like a river enters a delta region, and they sometimes feel lost for a time. Our task is to be delta boat pilots so that this results not in the loss of faith but in the development of a stronger faith. As described in Proverbs 11:2, "When pride comes, so does shame, but wisdom brings humility" (CEB). Our faculties seek to build that kind of wisdom.*

# Grant Us Courage

*I wish wisdom was sufficient, but the other essential virtue necessary for faithful leadership is courage. It might seem that courage simply comes with wisdom. We tend to think if students read Dietrich Bonhoeffer's* **The Cost of Discipleship** *they will absorb the lesson. But wisdom is knowing the difference between the way things are now and the way things are meant to be in the kingdom of God, while courage is the ability to move from one to the other.*

Consider the courage it takes for a pastor to walk into the room of someone who is dying, to evangelize the unchurched, or just to stand up every Sunday morning to speak. But what about the courage it takes to preach the unpopular word? Or the courage to stand up to the chair of the Staff-Parish Relations Committee on a matter of principle, even though she is the church's biggest donor? Or the courage to intervene with the alcoholic father of one of the kids in the youth group? Or what about the courage it takes to lead a congregation into the public square to confront issues like racism and economic injustice, immigration, prison reform, or the health-care system?

It takes courage to change. It takes courage to risk. And so courage is essential for leadership. As C. S. Lewis said, "Courage isn't simply one of the virtues, but the form of every virtue at the testing point."[4] I have learned that in the practice, usually the failures, of being a seminary CEO.

One example of both courage and a failure of courage is found in one of the most important documents in American history, Martin Luther King Jr.'s *Letter from a Birmingham Jail*.[5] While jailed for nonviolent protest of segregation, King wrote the letter describing his reasons for engaging in civil disobedience. The most telling thing about the letter is that it was addressed to pastors who saw themselves as enlightened moderates. King wrote to them:

The Negro's great stumbling block in his stride toward freedom isn't the White Citizen's Counciler or the Ku Klux Klanner, but the white moderate, who is more devoted to order than to justice.[6]

## How to Foster Courage

In *What Makes a Hero: The Surprising Science of Selflessness*, Elizabeth Svoboda surveys what we know. She finds "heroism and altruism are hues in a single broad spectrum of generosity,"[7] meaning the issue is how we become more generous of our time, our talent, our treasure, and our lives. It's probably not surprising that heroes are made, not born, and that role models are important.

Her most important finding is that courage is developed in groups who develop empathy for each other. I have learned a lot about this from Wesley Seminary's contact with the military, especially the military chaplains in a specialized Doctor of Ministry program. General James "Hoss" Cartwright is a retired four-star Marine general who serves on the Wesley Seminary Board. Cartwright lectures in my leadership class for the chaplains. He talks about how the military trains for bravery. He says, "I can scare you into the reflex to follow orders." That was how it used to be done. But now the process is very different. The training is designed around not letting your peer group down. Cartwright says that in basic training you learn you can't get through on your own, so you feel what he calls "peer pressure." It sounds to me like loyalty, even love.

This training contributes to resiliency, a quality that has become very important in a protracted war that has lasted over fifteen years. Svoboda talks about the very real phenomenon of "post traumatic growth," which often emerges in a group that has developed resilient bonds. The war correspondent Sebastian

Junger, in his book *Tribe: On Homecoming and Belonging*, describes how important group support is for soldiers. The problem of post-traumatic stress disorder is often the struggle of coming home to a divided and anxious society. Junger says, "Today's veterans often come home to find that, although they're willing to die for their country, they're not sure how to live for it."[8]

Communication technology raises interesting challenges. One military chaplain told of being in an operations tent in Iraq while mortar fire was coming in. Yet the soldier next to him was on the phone with his wife, talking about their mortgage. The point is, even though contact with home is a comfort, it interferes with group cohesion. In a similar way, social media promises to build a more global community, but more often it reinforces existing bias by walling off cyber neighborhoods and making people more frightened and defensive without the support of real human community.

The application of Christian theology to this research on courage seems obvious. The military chaplains speak of *esprit de corps*, which contains the word *spirit*. Their basic training is called the *crucible*, a word that has its origin in *crux*, a lamp hung before a devotional cross. And, of course, the very word *courage* is rooted in the original Latin word for *heart*. And the key to the formation of courage is the bonds that form in human community among those who covenant with each other as they pursue a common mission.

The sermon writes itself, but how do we apply it to our context? It seems clear that courage is more emotional than cognitive. Recall the concept of "well-differentiated leadership" described in the Introduction. Rabbi Friedman says such a leader is someone who "has clarity about his or her own life goals, and, therefore, someone who is less likely to become lost in the anxious emotional processes swirling about."[9]

We can understand this within the larger frame of the call to ministry. Vocational formation is the formation of courage. As Will Willimon says in his book *Calling and Character: Virtues of the Ordained Life,*

> The great ethical danger for clergy isn't that we might "burn out" to use a metaphor that is popular in our time, not that we might lose the energy required to do ministry. Our danger is that we might "black out," that is lose consciousness of why we are here and who we are called to be for Christ and his church.[10]

# The Seminary as a Community of Formation

To me, one of the most interesting implications of the research on courage is how the challenge for seminary faculty is much the same as the challenge for pastors. We may think the key is what we say from the pulpit or lectern, or what we write in the Pastor's Corner in the newsletter or on the website, or for that matter what I as seminary CEO write in an appeal letter. But in my experience, the quality of the stewardship Sunday sermon has very little to do with the ultimate generosity of the congregation. The same can be said for brilliant lectures as well as prophetic sermons. Our proclamations are important, but the formation of a disciple as well as a pastor has more to do with building relationships and community and how that work is connected to our shared mission and vision. This involves coaching, mentoring, reminding, encouraging, and holding accountable.

Disciples are formed in community. Clergy do this work
through ongoing, everyday encounters—through fellowship and
fundraising events, church meetings, casual conversations in the
narthex and fellowship hall, hospital visits, crisis interventions,
weddings, and funerals. In The United Methodist Church, people
speak a lot now about holy conferencing as a means of grace. But
the real holy conversations are not the morning before a vote.
They happen on the trellis of relationships built over years at the
seminary, in the congregation, and among the clergy.

*At the seminary, relational capital is built in the physical
community of the seminary, in conversations after class, in the
dining room, and in the chapel service. Courage comes from
this kind of eye-to-eye coaching and team building with others
who are preparing to answer their call. Perhaps as much as
a third of the work of seminary professors is in this personal,
time-intensive coaching of students. These relationships are
the incubators of wisdom and courage.*

A stained glass window in Wesley Seminary's chapel displays
this verse of scripture: "Therefore take the whole armor of God,
that you may be able to withstand in the evil day, and having done
all, to stand" (Eph 6:13 NRSV). I write this after a large white
supremacist rally in Charlottesville, Virginia, as I scan the news
reports anxiously, concerned for the safety of our students and
alumni who went to Charlottesville to participate peacefully in the
counterprotest. I am proud of them, and I know they are preparing
to preach about it in a few hours. But I also know it's going to take
more courageous congregations and more courageous pastors to
make real change in something as deep as racism. It takes courage
to change ourselves, let alone confront evil in our communities.

**93**

I've devoted a lot of time describing the formation of wisdom and courage because it's highly relevant to current pressures and trends in theological education. These virtues are formed in community, with fellow students and scholars. (Consider the "Flourishing in Ministry" research on the formation of identity in chapter 3). Something important is lost when people preparing for ministry don't "go away" to seminary, or when too much is taught and learned in front of a computer screen. While necessity may be the mother of invention, convenience isn't always a virtue.

> *There are some, especially in larger churches, arguing they should "grow their own" pastoral leaders. I frequently hear annual conference officials say it's important to keep pastors near their home or church, even though these will be itinerating clergy. I say in response, John the Baptist, and even Jesus himself, had to leave home and go to the wilderness. As a church, we have a long-term interest in preparing pastors to be self-differentiated, wise, and courageous leaders. As every farmer says, "Don't eat your seed corn."*

## The Promise and Limits of Online Learning

There isn't anything magical about the master of divinity degree as it's currently constituted in fourteen-week semesters. There's also nothing essential about long lectures and short question-and-answer periods. When it comes to online technology, after a period of resistance, United Methodist faculty are now fully embracing the benefits of online technology, and our seminaries are making extraordinarily expensive investments in hardware, software, and training so that this is of the highest quality.

We are finding online learning tools very useful. The technology helps us reach students with different learning styles, and we are incorporating artistic and non-textual elements, as we do in physical classrooms. Indeed, some of our faculty are learning to teach more effectively through technology. Recently, Professor Sathi Clarke shared his experience in an educational technology class taken by our faculty:

> Who says old dogs can't learn new tricks! Well into my third decade as a theological teacher, the online training course has provided an opportunity to assess and alter my teaching for a new cadre of students.... Up to this point, I have been a "content-centered" course designer. I worked hard to put together a comprehensive curriculum covering all the themes I wanted students to understand and assimilate. I am discovering how to become a "learning-focused" course designer.[11]

Here's what I hope we agree on. A purely online master of divinity is a necessary compromise for those who simply can't ever be part of the seminary community—for example, international students, especially with current obstacles from American immigration policies. Also, some courses are being offered online by United Methodist schools for United Methodist students in non–United Methodist seminaries or in special topics not offered at other schools.

*I think the future of the master of divinity will include, for many students in many of our seminaries, the use of online tools to deliver content combined with periods of time together in community to form both wisdom and courage. This is sometimes referred to as a "hybrid" approach, where online tools deliver content but intense periods of time between students and faculty provide the opportunity for self-differentiation. In fact, one could argue this helps us return to the ideal relationship*

*between student and teacher, the classic image of Socrates under
a tree posing questions to students who come prepared to debate
and struggle.*

The use of online tools requires clarity about what we are trying to accomplish and focused attention on community-building
and the formation of wisdom and courage as the virtues of pastoral identity. It should not be undertaken with the idea of saving
money.[12]

## Seminary Communities Are the Nurseries of the Church

"Seed bed" is one meaning of the word *seminary.* Where are
the leaders of the church a decade from now? Eighty percent are
on seminary campuses or in the databases of our seminaries and
are known to our recruiters and admissions officers.

Almost twenty-five years ago, Wesley Seminary coined the
phrase "culture of call" as we worked with the church to find the
next generation of clergy. At the time, the denomination was pro-
jecting a shortage of clergy. Our Culture of Call initiative urged
youth ministers, campus ministers, pastors, Sunday school teachers, and others to encourage young people to listen to God's call
in their lives. I preached many ministry Sunday sermons in various churches. The results have been extraordinary, even years later,
as many entering students say they first thought about ministry
because of our efforts years ago.

*Our challenge is to find the best young people to pursue
full-time ministry. The key is to remind ourselves continually
that we are not recruiting applicants for a job. We are like Eli,*

*helping Samuel hear the voice of God in his life (1 Sam 3).*
*This takes time. And seminaries are an indispensable partner*
*to the church in continuing to foster this culture of call.*

# Diversity as a Means of Grace

Focusing on the formative aspect of seminary education is more important now than ever. For fifty years seminaries have focused on fixing the problems we encounter while forming people for ministry. Before the mid-1960s, everyone who came to seminary was a young white male who was clear about his professional track. You could say they arrived pre-formed in the shape of the ministry as it had been for decades, or at least ready to be formed by a largely all-white, all-male faculty. Then everything started to change with increasing enrollments of African Americans and women, followed by second-career students. With this shift came an increase in theological diversity and questions others had not thought or dared to ask. And most of these "new" students had to work part-time or full-time jobs to afford seminary.

These students were coming out of an increasingly complex culture with a variety of different understandings about their calls to ministry. Some were "seekers" because they weren't sure what they were going to do. Seminaries worked at varying speeds to accommodate these new developments. That included diversifying the faculty and changing course scheduling for part-time students. Like a committee of cooks trying to figure out why the old recipe wasn't working anymore, seminaries made curricular revisions and produced a variety of soul-searching books to figure out how to make theological education work.

The mainline Protestant seminaries, with United Methodists in the lead, eventually embraced this diversity faster and more completely than the conservative evangelical seminaries. This came at a cost. It's simply harder to accommodate so many different people and ideas. Recruitment, curriculum design, teaching, student affairs, alumni affairs, and fundraising are all much easier if everyone is the same.

We have all come to realize this diversity is our strength, but it's harder to achieve. And we are wise enough to know we haven't figured it all out yet. But see this as an essential resource to deal with the issue of race, the single most important enduring issue in America. Students at United Methodist seminaries encounter greater personal challenge than if they were to go to the much more homogenous non–United Methodist seminaries in our region. Our seminaries have discovered our diverse communities are a means of grace. This is to say, we believe the Holy Spirit is working powerfully through our diversity.

Tropical rainforests are said to contain in their fertile genetic diversity the secret to the treatment of diseases. Similarly, seminaries are the one place in the church with the "biodiversity" to explore future possibilities.

*Traditional seminary education is innovative because in our midst are the variety of seeds and the fertile space for incubating the new ideas necessary to prepare students for a multicultural world. And in this community we provide the wisdom and courage necessary for leadership.*

*Chapter 6*

# SEMINARIES ARE THE SOLUTION, PART 2

## A New Seminary for the Twenty-First Century

Dan Aleshire, retired Chief Executive Officer of the Association of Theological Schools, said once:

> ATS schools have not been asleep at the switch, but the world around them has changed faster and perhaps more pervasively than the schools have. Ultimately, realities beyond the schools will require even more fundamental shifts in institutional form and educational character.[1]

Everyone is clear about the changes to which Dan was referring. Seminaries are experiencing the perfect storm: declining church membership, prolonged economic recession, criticism of the value (cost/benefit) of higher education in general, and online education. No one in the room during his speech would have been surprised if it started raining toads. And now, several years later, there are fewer people in the room.

I'm so invested in seminary education that I'm sure all this is our fault. If we'd only done a better job preparing pastors for

**99**

the past sixty years, our churches would be thriving with many new millennials joining by profession of faith. Churches would be leading voices for peace and justice; racism would be down, charity up; education would be valued, and the earth would be cooling.

*More than ever, I believe graduate theological education is vital but not sufficient for the revitalization of the church. We have to do more, we have to do better, and we have to become something different, something new. The goal is to be a new seminary that prepares a new, missional church.*

Many of our seminaries are already addressing the challenges I list below. I am bringing together a number of issues our seminary CEOs discuss regularly.

# I. We Must Do More

## A. Apologetics

We need more research in Christian apologetics. We often refer to scholarship as research, but that doesn't mean faculty wear lab coats or are out in the field looking for the lost ark like Indiana Jones. Instead, some work on primary research, which breaks new intellectual ground. More often, their work is like lawyers writing legal briefs as they dig deep into the text and tradition of the church and make the best case for ways to understand and practice the Christian faith. Sabbaticals and low course loads encourage this kind of scholarship, adding significantly to seminary expenditures. But we believe it's worth it.

*Apologetics* doesn't mean having to say we're sorry for being a Christian. Quite the opposite, it's the branch of theology that presents a reasoned defense of Christianity, especially to both skeptics and those who know nothing about the faith. Apologetics prepares clergy to engage an indifferent and even hostile mission field.

### 1. The Nature of the Authority of the Bible

Three areas of research are important right now. One is in the nature and authority of the Bible. Most United Methodists are not biblical literalists. More than a million participants in the boomer generation experienced Disciple Bible Studies (1987ff) and now Covenant Bible Study (2014),[2] which instills an appreciation for the rich complexity, mystery, and incongruities of biblical interpretation. So how does homosexuality, an issue barely mentioned in seven passages, become a test of biblical authority? I think it is because it raises, for many people, deeper questions about the Bible and its interpretation. This is what we should be addressing with the goal of a deeper and more durable faith.

### 2. Science and Religion

Similarly, the ongoing debate about evolution and global warming in many of our churches suggests the need for more resources in science and religion. The real questions are not about the age of the universe or whether we share the same ancestors as the apes or whether the world is in God's hands. The urgent theological issue is not the origin of the species; it is the destiny of humanity.

The false choice is often set up as science or religion. The third way is to discover the wondrous synergy of science and religion. Thinking about this is like entering an intellectual delta region. As Alice says in Wonderland, "It gets curiouser and curiouser."

But curiosity is a gift from God, and the fruit of asking questions is the realization from Psalm 19:1: "The heavens are telling the glory of God."[3]

### 3. Interfaith Dialogue

The third issue for our time is what Christians should think of other faiths. Of course, 9/11 focused attention on this question. One approach is to compare religions as if they are cultural phenomena. Another approach is like my first class in world religions, which might as well have been called "Why Christianity Is the Best Religion."

At Wesley Seminary, we have been working on a third way to engage with people of other faiths. The overarching question is: How can we be true to our faith and fully engaged in the world? Our faculty work to construct a missional theology that empowers the church to be both confident and humble in mission, recognizing the intrinsic spiritual value of other people and other faiths.[4]

This kind of research in Christian apologetics helps the church find the third way between false choices and helps us be confident and gracious addressing the most critical issues of our time.

## B. Practices of Missional Leaders

### 1. Prepare More Effective and Confident Public Theologians

Many pastors, often in suburban and rural congregations, are reluctant to address important issues of the day and view any controversial issue as the third rail of ministry. They fear loss of money and members, and they often develop a kind of pastoral rationale for avoiding controversy. Meanwhile, many pastors, often in urban areas, understand part of their role *is* to have a robust prophetic voice. Of course, this is a generalization, but as Hollifield documented, this general urban/rural pattern was true in America at the turn of the last century as well.[5] This was the period when modern graduate theological schools were established in the growing cities to help their graduates engage the new urban and industrialized society.

Christians everywhere in every generation have recognized the public implications of their faith. Methodists have a long history of theology in public, beginning with John Wesley. He raised a strong public voice about a number of issues, including slavery, prison reform, and the Corn Laws, which involved taxation policy and substance abuse.

This isn't a difference between religious liberals and conservatives. For instance, Doug Strong in *Perfectionist Politics* describes the role conservative evangelical churches, seeking entire sanctification, played to oppose slavery.[6] An increasing number of pastors in every region are now sensing the need to preach about global warming, health-care, the opiod crisis, and the enduring issue of American life—racism.

Sondra Wheeler describes a critical role of the clergy as "moral theologians in residence." She describes how this role is expressed in preaching, teaching, counseling, and in the character of the pastor himself or herself.[7]

Wesley Seminary is particularly interested in this area of ministry because of our location. We are nonpartisan but not disinterested in the great issues of the day. We intend that every graduate of our seminary acquires the wisdom, grace, and skill to help congregations deal with controversy in a non-anxious fashion.[8]

### 2. Help Clergy Learn How to Do Good Well

In the 1950s, as modern psychology was becoming professionalized, seminaries and clergy saw this as a vital new skill for ministry. Soon courses appeared in pastoral care, and the church began to require these courses for ordination. In significant ways, pastors became therapists, though amateur in the level of their preparation.

Now great advances have been made at the intersection of economics, management, and the social sciences. In the past, congregations engaged in mission projects both home and abroad in an ad hoc and often ineffective manner. For example, youth groups in our area of the country regularly go to Appalachia on mission trips. While there must be hundreds of coats of paint on houses in parts of West Virginia, the level of poverty has not changed.

The professor and evangelist Tony Campolo once said to me, "They don't go there to do good; they go there to feel good." There is some truth to that. Certainly, this is still a criticism in what was once called the "foreign mission field." The new face of colonialism is referred to as "mission tourism."

But now we have the opportunity for clergy to develop insights into effective missional practices similar to the way in which they learn about effective counseling. This orientation includes an awareness of how to network with those governmental and nongovernmental agencies who can be the best partners and an exploration into the systemic causes of societal ills.

Kyunglim Shin-Lee's important book in the field of international mission work has the English title *Missionary Power, Urgent Inspection of Korean Mission.*[9] The Korean Church is well-known for its passionate, sacrificial dedication to world mission. But until the research of Shin-Lee and her collaborators, there had not been serious evaluations of the effectiveness of that work, including a failure to listen to the voices of the indigenous people. This research will enable the largest missional churches in the world to do good well.

### 3. Tap the Potential of the Laity

This book focuses on the clergy and clergy preparation. But it's the unpaid lay people on our seminary Board of Governors who are the key to our success and faithfulness. When we say we need to "empower the laity," that phrase sounds like a top-down delegation of a finite amount of power and authority.

Instead, let me offer a metaphor. Before there were personal computers in the 1980s, there was a single computer (the mainframe), which was the source of all the information and decision-making. All the other devices depended on that one computer. In fact, screens were called dumb terminals. Today, my cellphone has more capability than that mainframe did. And all the computers are networked together. There are still vast farms of computers that form the hubs of this rich network. These are called "servers," which is a helpful metaphor for shared leadership and visioning. Let's call it "server leadership."

Server leadership is hard for those who have the title of The Reverend or President. But if I read the story of Pentecost correctly, the Holy Spirit fell on everyone. And we know from organizations as formerly rigid as the military, organizational structures are becoming flatter, knowledge is shared, and power—the ability and energy to do things—comes from the multiplying effect of everyone committed to the mission.

105

# II. We Must Do Better

Every organization has a strength that is also its weakness. For seminaries, it's our instinct that "perfect makes practice," rather than the other way around. We assume that if we can just think deep enough about the Bible, our history, and our theology, this intellectual reflection will remove error and result in effective ministry.

The result is something the German theologian Helmut Thielicke described years ago in his book *A Little Exercise for Young Theologians*: "This is true of the theological student...the inner muscular strength of a young Christian is horribly squeezed to death in the formal armor of abstract ideas."[10] The increasingly esoteric knowledge of the theological academic guilds both baffles the laity and leaves no space in the curriculum for the development of effective practice.

## A. Improve as Teachers

Faculty love to teach, but they are often not formally trained to teach. For the most part, future professors learn by watching their professors and through student teaching. If they land a job in a tenure-track position, their teaching is observed once or twice by their colleagues, and their student evaluations are reviewed prior to their advancement to tenure. The United Methodist schools that offer PhD programs now include some courses in the art of teaching. By contrast, to be a middle school science teacher, my son-in-law, Dave, took twelve courses in learning theory and practice and two semesters of intensely supervised internship.

We support our faculty to become more highly skilled teachers.[11] The process of creating online courses involves learning some new skills in teaching. Seminaries are required by accrediting standards to measure whether students are learning by assessing outcomes, as contrasted with traditional assessment of process; and we are required to measure the success rates of our alumni as never before.

These developments are having a positive effect on teaching. But we are not there yet, and we may need more fundamental improvement. My colleague Ann Michel, Associate Director of the Lewis Leadership Center and editor of the online resource *Leading Ideas*, has studied congregational ministries extensively and concludes we need to change the way we teach:

> I think churches and seminaries both operate out of a paradigm that says people learn the Christian faith by sitting in the pew, listening to someone talk, and maybe going to some classes or groups. It's a paradigm of formation that really isn't working anymore. It assumes people already understand the faith before they come in the door, or they are at least pre-programmed culturally to think seeking faith is important. This paradigm of faith formation is particularly ill-suited to non-traditional expressions of Christian community. I think we need to reexamine from the ground up our assumptions about spiritual formation and our clergy need to be equipped to form people in faith in radically different ways.[12]

The opportunity for seminaries is this: if we can practice new ways to teach, this will, in turn, be a model for those who preach and teach in congregations. Change starts with us.

## B. Redesign the Teaching of the Practices of Ministry

What do we know about how our clergy are doing as practitioners? Feedback is essential for growth. Notice how the most accomplished athletes and artists—even as they are setting new standards for excellence in their fields—have coaches, teachers, and colleagues they look to for feedback. The 360-degree feedback method is one of the most helpful ways for good leaders to become better as employer, employee, and colleagues offer mutual constructive feedback.

The Lewis Pastoral Leadership Inventory[13] (LPLI) provides a 360-degree instrument for feedback based on the practices of pastoral leadership. There are many fine secular inventories, but we found that the questions did not match well what clergy do.

Many denominations and United Methodist annual conferences have made major commitments to define, assess, and improve clergy effectiveness. Most have developed a list of characteristics or practices of effective pastoral leadership. Drawing from their work, the Center developed three categories for evaluation in the LPLI: character (who the leader is), competence (what the leader knows and does), and contribution (what the leader accomplishes).

After nearly three thousand clergy have completed the LPLI, some observations emerge:

- On questions related to character (especially matters of spiritual authenticity and integrity) and competence (certain discrete ministry skills such as preaching or teaching), both pastors and observers place these qualities in the higher rank.

- Pastors rank the lowest in questions related to the contribution category (what a pastor accomplishes). This includes accomplishments related to worship attendance, stewardship, and faith formation. It's worth noting agreement. Clergy confess they are not doing as well on these measures, and the laity confirm their estimates.

So how can we improve these scores and be more effective in teaching the practices of ministry? One obstacle is the crowded master of divinity curricula. Seminarians are not required to study religion before seminary. So they must first take a number of introductory courses in the classic theological disciplines in addition to upper-level seminars. This limits the number of courses in the practice of ministry.

Preaching, worship, and pastoral care naturally get slots in our curricula, and there is usually a course in Christian education or formation and evangelism. But a whole range of skills in management, leadership, finance, group dynamics, legal accountability, conflict management, community organizing, and facilities management must be studied collectively in one course if they are mentioned at all.

All seminaries have a field education requirement, usually involving supervised work in a congregation. But that area of the seminary curriculum has evolved to focus on what is termed *praxis*. This simply means reflection on practice, which is meant to integrate academic theology with the practices of ministry. This is important, but it isn't the same as learning the skills of the practice of ministry.

Thus if a seminary graduate appears not to know how to run a church, it's because the necessary skills haven't been taught. One part of the solution is to find a way to create more space in the master of divinity curriculum for more skills-based courses and more frequent and intensive supervised practice.

However, students can't learn the practices of ministry solely in the master of divinity program. There isn't enough room in the curriculum. But more importantly, the teachable moment for the practices of ministry is after the first seminary degree.

For example, let's consider preaching. Malcolm Gladwell, in *Outliers: The Story of Success*,[14] famously cites research that it requires ten thousand hours of practice to become exceptional in any professional skill, from surgery to chess. But others have argued this is valid only if you have some way to gauge how you are doing. A seminary student probably preaches four professionally critiqued sermons plus two more in the ordination process. What about when they are in ministry?

Let's do the math. Gladwell's ten thousand hours achieve what he calls "world class" level. Let's cut that in half to aim for being only "good." If we include twenty hours of weekly preparation time, that means it takes about five years preaching every Sunday to reach the hours needed. If pastors received careful feedback on their sermons, not just the handshake at the end of the service, then they would have an easier time becoming good preachers. Few clergy ever have that opportunity.

I think this means that seminaries not only have to do something more and do some things better, it means we have to become something different.

## III. We Have to Become Something New

Presently, our thirteen United Methodist seminaries are graduate theological schools offering the master of divinity for clergy. We each offer other degree and non-degree programs, but the master of divinity has been our core mission and is the key to our business model. Setting aside the ludicrously arrogant name of the degree, it should be clear from the foregoing that modifying this curriculum can only go so far, and it's a zero-sum game.

Justo Gonzalez, in his history of theological education, reminds us that clergy education has not always been done this way.

> We must realize that the relationship between study and ordination isn't as clear-cut as we have made it. Throughout most of the history of the church, even the highest levels of theological education have not necessarily led to ordination, and ordination has often preceded advanced studies. The best theological study is motivated primarily not by the need to satisfy requirements for ordination but by the love of God.[15]

# Centers of Comprehensive Theological Education

> *We need to imagine how seminaries can think about how to be missional ourselves and begin to modify the graduate school master of divinity business and become centers for comprehensive theological education for the whole church.*

Consider three challenges to be met and three models we might borrow. The challenges are

1.  The need to offer skills-based training well beyond graduate education.

2.  The need to offer seminary education to the pastors of nearly half of all United Methodist congregations who are not able to enroll in masters-level programs.[16]

3.  The need to penetrate deeper into congregations, through the laity, with high-quality theological education and research.

111

Potential models to emulate are

1.  Extension programs like the agricultural extension
    programs established in state land-grant universities
    by the 1887 Hatch Act, which helped family farmers
    greatly improve their techniques by sharing successful
    strategies.

2.  The health-care system whereby the categories of pro-
    fessionally trained medical professionals has greatly
    increased.

3.  The business school where the MBA is still central, but
    the faculty and programs have greatly expanded to fill
    niches in continuing executive education.

Many seminaries currently offer programs borrowing from
some or all of these models. In our case, we have the Course of
Study School for local pastors, we offer continuing clergy education through the Lewis Leadership Center,[17] and we offer online
adult lay education courses.[18] But we are envisioning much more
extensive offerings to serve pastors, congregations, and annual
conferences in our region.

There are two significant threshold questions:

1.  How can we extend the value of a seminary education,
    not just the knowledge, also the formation in wisdom
    and courage and the benefit of a community of diver-
    sity as discussed in chapter 5, to those not receiving the
    master of divinity?

2.  How can we overcome the problem of the low "price
    point" for clergy and lay education described in chapter 1?

Bishop Ken Carter recently described these two problems by describing it as a "mixed economy of church and pastoral leadership."[19] Seeing the opportunities, having some models, and knowing the barriers is halfway to a solution.

Consider the image of the delta region I offered in the introduction. Deltas are disorienting and contain some danger for the navigator. However, they are also fertile and full of new life. This delta region we find ourselves in is an opportunity to practice what we preach. Methodists are experimenters in grace, looking for the ways the Holy Spirit is moving.

Seminaries don't need to invent all the solutions. For instance, on the one hand, Lew Parks in *Small on Purpose*[20] shows how many small churches are quite durable and have things to teach us. On the other end of the spectrum, Jim Wind, retired Director of the Alban Institute, studied large membership churches (findings not yet published), showing that these churches, which greatly increased in number beginning in the 1970s, have been conducting their own experiments in missional activity and small group forms of discipleship.

The role of a new kind of seminary as a center for comprehensive theological education isn't only to generate knowledge but to aggregate and disseminate best practices to help form a new kind of church.

This means seminaries and the denomination need to arrive at a "new deal," a new contract between the various levels of the church. At the general church level, this involves the MEF and a way to reduce student debt nationally. At the annual conference level, it involves agreements to provide the best a seminary has to offer for various forms of ministry—full-time clergy, part-time clergy, and lay leadership. And at the local church level, we need a new arrangement with congregations to foster a culture of call and craft better ways both to financially support and apprentice ordained clergy and to extend coaching and mentoring opportunities into the early years of ministry after the master of divinity.

*C h a p t e r  7*

# ASSURANCE

As I write this, a reporter is covering Hurricane Irma and talking about that shifting place in the eye of the storm where there is stillness, a parting of the clouds, and blue sky. It's a fitting metaphor to describe the center of grace as the goal of a new kind of seminary and a renewed United Methodist Church. That stillness can't be frozen in place and time. It's always moving, as is the Holy Spirit itself. This is why we must always be adapting and moving ourselves toward that place.

Stephen Covey, in *7 Habits of Highly Effective People: Powerful Lessons in Personal Change,* recommended we "begin with the end in mind."[1] Our end is what Shakespeare's *Hamlet* called the "undiscovered country, from whose bourne, no traveler returns." For Christians, it isn't undiscovered. It's God's kingdom, and as Jesus said, it's nearby. It's the substance of salvation, and it's glimpsed in those moments when both who we are and what we do are in line (justified) with God's desire for creation. As John Wesley imagined it, it is, "Heaven, opened in the soul."

That experience is what we call *assurance.* It was the object of John Wesley's spiritual journey, what he called "true religion." Hal Knight describes what Wesley discovered in his grand experiment in grace: "True religion consists in having certain affections which are both capacities (enabling us to love) and dispositions (inclining us to love)."[2] Wesley described this assurance when he cited Hebrews 11:1: "Now faith is the assurance of things hoped for, the evidence or conviction of things not seen."[3]

As a leader, I seek that assurance. I try to be the non-anxious presence in an anxious time—the self-differentiated servant leader I described in the introduction. In the steps I take and the words I use, I try to find that balance between being the Bluebird of Happiness saying "everything's going to be all right" and Chicken Little saying "the sky is falling." I don't seek assurance that I'm doing the right thing; I am assured when those I am in ministry with are all trying to answer God's call—that we are seeking to be centered in grace.

## A Story of Two Fathers

Let me share the story behind my call. It is a true story of two fathers—my own father, Fred Wilson, and the father in the house next door. The family that lived next door to us when I was growing up was very troubled. When the kids were behaving like kids, the mother would pull out the secret weapon. She would use a phrase that maybe some of you remember. "Wait until your father gets home!" It was a warning, a threat.

That is one way of thinking about God. It's the way some people read the Bible. If that were my theology, I would be a little paranoid, always worried about whether I was okay with this God. Let's say you're a church with that kind of theology. Your mission is clear. You've got to warn people. Your job is to help people get saved, one by one, *from* a fate worse than death. There is a phrase used at Christmastime to describe that understanding of God entering the world: "You'd better watch out." It's strange how they can make the good news sound like bad news.

I don't think that's who we are as Methodists. Fortunately, I have my own father as a point of comparison. When my sisters and I were young we would hear the front screen door open and close around 6 o'clock. Do you know that sound? I can still hear it. Knowing it was my father coming home for supper, we would all shout something in unison. Do you know what it was? We shouted, "Daddy's home!" Daddy's home! It was a different spirit: it was good news.

We felt that way because we knew even if we had done things wrong that day, he would gather us in his arms and forgive us. The forgiveness was the key. That way of understanding God makes everything different. When we talk about this God entering our lives, it isn't a warning: it's good news. The message isn't "wait until your father gets home." There is another phrase used at Christmas time that describes that understanding of God entering the world. It's the message the angel gave to the shepherds. "Fear not, for behold, I bring you good news" (KJV).

When we shouted, "Daddy's home!" it meant that we were going to do something together. Maybe we would go and play catch, go get an ice cream cone, or go to the mountains. If that is the kind of father God is, then being called by this God to a discipleship matters in *this* world.

We are not a religion devoted to a distant creator or some mysterious supernatural force. Our God became part of this earth, part of human history. He walked out of the wilderness and called men and women to join his cause. He told the truth, he exposed hypocrisy, and he spoke of how life is meant to be lived. But he was subject to the laws of physics and the laws of the Roman Empire. He had both friends and enemies. He laughed and he cried. When you cut him, he bled, and when you killed him, he died.

God knows about evil. What God is doing is calling us to be a part of the solution. The solution is a promise; it's called the kingdom of God. It's a promise that one day there will be no more pain or suffering, no war or disease, and that even the power of death will be defeated. From beginning to end, the Bible glows with the hope that this kingdom will come, and it will happen in and through a chosen people who have a divine destiny.

Jesus began his ministry saying, "Change your hearts and lives! Here comes the kingdom of heaven!"(Matt 3:2 CEB). And for the next three years this kingdom was all he could talk about. He taught us to pray saying: "Thy kingdom come, thy will be done, on earth as it's in heaven." With his death and resurrection, this promise of salvation is made to the world through the life and the witness of those who call themselves by his name.

I travelled back to California in the middle of my first year of seminary to say goodbye to my mother, who was ending a long battle with cancer. As I left her hospital room she said, "Think of it as an adventure." I think she was talking both about her death and about my future.

*My hope and my vocation is to build a new seminary that serves a new church. But neither of those is the end we should have in mind. We believe in salvation. But as Methodists we don't just ask what we are saved from; we ask what we are saved for. Daddy's home. Think of it as an adventure. I believe heaven is a place in the mind of God where my mother and father are experiencing great joy. But it's also a new world order, coming on earth as it is in heaven. The church should have the end in mind that God has and be making the earth look more like heaven.*

# WESLEY THEOLOGICAL SEMINARY

**The New Church and The New Seminary**

## The Challenge of the Twenty-First Century

*The twenthy-first century is a time of a deep and urgent search for spiritual meaning and purpose.* The millennium opens in great turmoil and uncertainty: terrorism, war, plagues of biblical proportion, and some of the worst natural disasters in history. But it's also a time of great opportunity and spiritual revival. Advances in science, technology, finance, communications, and management make it possible to cure disease, bring peace among nations, be good stewards of the planet, send relief and resources anywhere on earth, and end extreme poverty. Where the need is greatest, the Christian movement is strongest and the Holy Spirit is most evident. God is at work offering hope in desperate places and calling us to accomplish the ancient biblical mandate to "proclaim the acceptable year of the Lord."

*The challenge to Christian disciples in this generation is to live the Great Commandment and the Great Commission on a global scale.*

Meeting this challenge will require hopeful people of character who practice Christian values such as compassion, forgiveness, generosity, justice, and humility. The world needs men and women who have the conviction and courage of their faith to lead sacrificial lives.

# The New Church

*These disciples come from a regeneration of the church.* Just as the gospel is always new, the church must always be reinventing itself as something new and redemptive in the world.

*The new church is mission-centered; it grows because it makes a difference in people's lives and it makes a difference in the world.* The new church is focused on being a part of God's mission in the world, not as something to do once the church is strong but as the source of its strength. Every congregation can become a new church by re-centering on mission.

*The new church is guided by a vision of the kingdom of God, led by the example of Jesus, and strengthened by the Holy Spirit.* It's hopeful and future-oriented; it's full of joy and a sense of purpose. It's relevant and global. It engages in the great issues of the day, seeking justice from the perspective of faith.

*The new church is the family of Christ* where burdens are shared, growth is celebrated, and people are prayed for by name. It's a worshiping community where the glorious mystery of God is experienced. It's a healing center where broken lives are put back together. It's a big tent where everyone is welcome and diversity is a source of truth and strength.

*The new church is confident in sharing its good news and gracious toward those of other faiths, knowing God seeks not judges or juries, but witnesses.* It's both grounded in scripture and unafraid of scientific discovery, ready to join in a discussion of the meaning and purpose of human life.

*The new church requires a change in the way we think about ministry.* In the new church, everyone is in ministry. The new ministry is mission-centered; we ask not what the church will do for us but what we can do to be a part of God's mission. In the new church, people constantly grow in grace, deepening spiritually in order to love God and neighbor with all their heart and soul and mind and to make a difference in God's world. Motivated by a strong experience of Jesus's call, these disciples pray, learn, and serve as a way of life.

*The new ministry requires excellence in leadership.* These leaders put it all together; they are compassionate, imaginative, courageous, and visionary. They must be able to walk into intensive care units and stand at gravesides and minister to people in their moments of greatest private, personal need. They also know the way from death to life, from meaninglessness to purpose. They lead congregations from the sanctuary to the world.

## The New Seminary

*The twenty-first century needs a new kind of seminary to help build the new church.* Before, seminaries prepared pastors to maintain healthy churches in stable neighborhoods. Now, every neighborhood is changing, and many churches are losing their members and their confidence. They long for a recovery of their sense of mission and a new kind of leadership. This is the challenge to seminaries. Wesley Theological Seminary is answering that challenge, building a new kind of seminary. Wesley is a place of mission-hearted people and mission-minded scholarship for a mission-centered church.

*The new seminary fosters hope and models courage; it cultivates wisdom and nurtures creativity.* Some see the tragedies of our time as "acts of God," or signs of God's judgment. We believe God is love and that Jesus saves and that the Holy Spirit is calling Christians to perform the true acts of God in the world: hospitality, mercy, rescue, and justice. Wesley's faculty helps form the deep center of thoughtful Christianity. Our goal is the mature faith that comes from in-depth study of the scripture and the historic teachings of the faith. We cherish that which is true and enduring in the tradition. And we are the research and development arm of the church, looking for the new ways the Holy Spirit is moving in the world. We value imagination with an approach to arts that is in service to the sacred.

*The new seminary is a holy community.* In a fragmented, fast-paced, and conflicted world, the new seminary seeks to be a model of what the new church can be. Wesley's student body and faculty are among the most diverse in theological education. We focus on fostering spiritual disciples in order to form a "communion in diversity" so that our students will become spiritually centered leaders.

*The new seminary is global and engages in the great issues of the day.* The new church world is fast and interconnected. Wesley is strategically positioned, and our faculty is eager to extend our reach and teach in new ways. We seek to be a part of what God is doing in the world. Wesley is placed in Washington, DC so that our students are at the crossroads of world affairs and our faculty are a resource to the opinion and policy shapers of the public square.

*The new seminary is church-based; it prepares leaders for the new church and is a resource for mission-centered congregations.* Theological education can no longer simply trickle down from a few ordained ministers. The new ministry is a variety of people in a variety of vocations and locations across the world. Wesley prepares both ordained and lay leadership through formal degree and certification programs. We offer point-of-need conferences and Internet resources, consultations with congregations and denominations, and programs in professional continuing education and lifelong disciple education for congregations. And we work with the church to identify the next generation of pastoral leaders.

*The new seminary expects excellence and cares about results.* The biblical measure of success is fruitfulness. Our goal is fruitful leadership for a mission-shaped church; we are successful if the graduates of our programs lead churches that are vital and engaged effectively in mission. The Wesley faculty helps students put it all together: faith and practice, knowledge and spirituality. Leaders in the new ministry preach and teach in ways that make faith relevant to life and life relevant to faith. They draw from twenty centuries of tradition and a variety of cultures to create authentic and exciting worship. They articulate a vision of the kingdom of God that guides the church into the world.

# THE VALUE OF SCHOLARSHIP FOR THEOLOGICAL EDUCATION

## A Statement from AUMTS for the Council of Bishops

### October 15, 2014

*"Be strong in the grace that is in Christ Jesus; and what you have heard from me through many faithful witnesses entrust to faithful people who will be able to teach others as well."*
—2 Timothy 2:1-2

*"United Methodist schools of theology share a common mission of preparing persons for leadership in the ministry of The United Methodist Church; of leading in the ongoing reflection on Wesleyan theology; and of assisting the church in fulfilling its mission to make disciples of Jesus Christ for the transformation of the world."*
—United Methodist Book of Discipline, ¶1422

# Why Does Scholarship Matter?

Why is it important for The United Methodist Church to have strong theological schools that nurture faculties who are committed to high standards of theological scholarship? Some people in the church today are skeptical about the value of high-level academic study. Indeed, in popular usage, the word "academic" can sometimes be used to mean "obscure, irrelevant, immaterial." To say "the question is academic," can mean, in some contexts, that it is a nitpicking or trivial question that should be of no concern to practical, sensible people. As the church faces many economic challenges and pressures, some voices are questioning whether we really need to invest all the time and trouble to send prospective pastors through three years of expensive, technical M.Div. courses taught by "high-powered" Ph.D.s; Couldn't we just hire skilled ministry practitioners to teach students how to be ministers? Couldn't we eliminate costly campuses and libraries and teach them everything they need to know in online certificate courses? Or, indeed, couldn't we just train future ministers in apprenticeship programs in successful churches, without requiring any sort of higher academic training at all? Why does scholarship matter, and why does having an academically excellent faculty matter?

In this moment of the church's history, we, the Deans and Presidents of the thirteen United Methodist theological schools, would like to highlight three key contributions of strong theological scholarship for the health and wellbeing of ministerial education. It is our hope that the bishops of the church will join us in supporting these contributions and fostering wider awareness in the churches of their importance. We also hope that the church will continue to challenge our schools and hold us accountable for providing not only the best of these particular contributions but also others essential to forming faithful and creative leaders for the church.

# Three Key Contributions of Theological Scholarship

### *Roots*

One key role of scholarship is to provide deep roots for the church. There is always a danger that the church will become conformed to the spirit of the age, flattened out by loss of historical perspective. But the patient work of theological scholarship gives the church roots, so that we are not, like many other institutions, "blown about by every wind of doctrine" (Eph 4:14). Serious scholarship gives us the long view; it enables us to have critical perspective on what our age regards as common sense.

In his essay "On the Reading of Old Books," C. S. Lewis explains the value of immersing ourselves deeply in the wisdom that comes from encountering older writings and traditions:

> Every age has its own outlook. It is specially good at seeing certain truths and specially liable to make certain mistakes. We all, therefore, need the books that will correct the characteristic mistakes of our own period. And that means the old books. . . .

And of course the old books from which we Christians particularly take our bearings are the books of the Old and New Testaments, along with the body of careful and passionate interpretation that has grown up around them over more than two millennia of close reading by faithful men and women in the church—including, for us, especially the men and women of the Wesleyan tradition. The scholars on our faculties have special expertise that enables us to reclaim and understand the traditions that we have received.

At the same time, it must be emphasized that historically grounded study does not confine us to the past; rather, it provides deep roots that can *nurture* the church, even in times of stress and

drought. Understanding Scripture in its original historical context—
and, as John Wesley emphasized, in the original languages—as well as
understanding how it has been read across the centuries by the saints,
can help us to grow in healthy continuity with the tradition. Likewise,
understanding the life of Christian people as they have related with
God and expressed their faith over time can also help us understand,
claim, and reshape the tradition as people continue to experience,
discern, and follow God in the present age.

Scholarship itself has its fads and trends, of course, so there is
nothing magic in academic work, no foolproof cure for confinement
to the shallow assumptions of the present moment. But scholars who
are well trained will always lead us back to drink freshly from the
fountain of the Word, and over time this will promote correction of
aberrations and healthy growth.

### Vision

At the same time, sound scholarship does not only look back to
the past. It also reflects critically and imaginatively on the present
and helps us chart a course for the future. We do not merely *repeat*
the tradition; we *recover* it for our time, discovering fresh ways in
which Scripture and the church's time-tested wisdom can speak to
new occasions, new challenges, and ways that the tradition contin-
ues to emerge as Christians experience the continuing movements
of the Holy Spirit in the world. Discerning the richness of tradition
requires not only deep knowledge, but also skillful and disciplined
imagination. The best scholarship engages in what Ellen Davis has
called "critical traditioning."[1] Tradition is an ongoing dialogue between the past and present with openness to God's future. Study of
the past enables us to see the present in a new light, to diagnose its

1. E. F. Davis, "Critical Traditioning: Seeking an Inner Biblical Hermeneutic,"
in E. F. Davis and R. B. Hays (eds.), *The Art of Reading Scripture* (Grand Rapids:
Eerdmans, 2003), 163-180.

ills and to imagine its healing transformation. Study of the present enables us to reflect deeply on Christian life in the world, seeking to discern the movements of the Holy Spirit amid contemporary global complexities, which reveal God and God's will for creation anew.

The scholars on the faculties of our thirteen theological schools are actively engaged in creative and critical reflection on the challenges of our time, including (for example) new styles and patterns of worship, care of the environment, the church's understanding of race and gender, changing patterns of human community shaped by new technologies, the church's engagement with health care, and the changing relationship of the church to political institutions in a pluralistic, post-Constantinian era. The church greatly benefits from the careful, reflective wisdom that grows out of fresh scholarly work in all fields of study in interactive relationship.

### Character

The discipline of serious scholarship contributes to the formation of character in the church's leaders. Anyone who has studied the Christian tradition carefully understands how complex human experience is, and, even more, how mysterious is the God we serve. Real scholarship therefore discourages hasty and superficial judgments. It encourages patient and sympathetic probing not only of the meaning of texts, not only of the past, but also of the motives of those we encounter in the present. Real scholarship promotes *a hermeneutic of charity* that seeks to understand the mind and motives of people and cultures that may initially seem strange to us.

The greatest scholars are usually (not always, but usually) also the most gracious and thoughtful people, the most patiently curious in engaging students and colleagues. They are not arrogant self-promoters, because they seek above all to learn and to understand the object of their study. And when the object of the study is Scripture or the history of God's people, the close scrutiny of it can often promote intellectual humility—or even the fruit of the Spirit.

Of course, these generalizations have their exceptions. Of course there are scholars who can be narrow, petty, or self-absorbed. But if one is studying St. Francis or John Wesley or Jesus, it is hard to resist the pull of their example towards holiness, generosity, and passion for justice.

So in our time, when popular culture, even in the church, can be heedless of the past and dominated by shrill polemic, deep scholarship can help the church's leaders become wiser and more humane people.

# Forming "Faithful People Who Will Be Able to Teach Others"

At the end of Matthew's Gospel, the disciples encounter the risen Jesus on a mountain in Galilee. He charges them to "Go and make disciples of all nations, baptizing them in the name of the Father and of the Son and of the Holy Spirit, and teaching them to obey everything I have commanded you" (Matt 28:19-20a). Just as they have been taught by Jesus, they are to teach others. Just as they have been made into disciples by Jesus' example and instruction, so they too are to pursue the vocation of making more disciples.

That is a picture of the mission of the faculties of our theological schools. At the end of the day, a community of scholarship is nothing more nor less than a community of people who have been rigorously taught and who seek now to share rigorously with others the treasure that has been given to them. Our theological schools seek not only to train pastors how to do their work faithfully but also to train future faculty members for the ministry of teaching, both in in the theological schools and in other Christian institutions. To renew the church, we need strong academic leaders who are committed to the task of making disciples.

To build an excellent theological faculty is nothing more nor less than to gather a team of disciples who are rooted in the tradition they have received, animated by a vision of making disciples of all nations, and formed by the character of the Lord they have followed. That task of making disciples is of course given to all the church's leaders. But our theological schools have a special vocation to respond to Jesus' commission by informing and forming the mind of the church. As we seek to carry out that commission, we trust that the One who promised to be with us will empower and sustain our work.

Mary Elizabeth Moore, Boston University School of Theology

Jan Love, Candler School of Theology, Emory University

Jeffrey Kuan, Claremont School of Theology

Javier Viera, Drew University Theological School

Richard Hays, Duke Divinity School, Duke University

Albert Mosley, Gammon Theological Seminary

Lallene J. Rector, Garrett-Evangelical Theological Seminary

Thomas V. Wolfe, Iliff School of Theology

Jay Rundell, Methodist Theological School in Ohio

William Lawrence, Perkins School of Theology, Southern Methodist University

H. Sharon Howell, Saint Paul School of Theology

Wendy J. Deichmann, United Theological Seminary

David McAllister-Wilson, Wesley Theological Seminary

# NOTES

## Preface

1. To learn more about the programs in the Institute for Community Engagement, visit https://www.wesleyseminary.edu/ice /about-us/overview-2/.

2. The United Methodist seminaries are: Boston University School of Theology (www.bu.edu/STH); Candler School of Theology of Emory University (www.candler.emory.edu); Claremont School of Theology (https://cst.edu); Drew University Theological School (www.drew.edu/theological-school/); Duke University Divinity School (www.divinity.duke.edu); Garrett-Evangelical Theological Seminary (www.garrett.edu); Iliff School of Theology (www .iliff.edu); Interdenominational Theological Center (www.itc.edu); Methodist Theological School in Ohio (www.mtso.edu); Perkins School of Theology, Southern Methodist University (www.smu.edu /perkins); Saint Paul School of Theology (www.spst.edu); United Theological Seminary (www.united.edu); and Wesley Theological Seminary (www.wesleyseminary.edu).

## Introduction

1. Robin Gill, *Churchgoing and Christian Ethics* (Cambridge, UK: Cambridge University Press, 1999), 82.

2. John Wesley, "Sermon II—The Almost Christian," in *The Works of the Rev. John Wesley, A.M.,* ed. John Emory (New York: Carlton & Lanahan, 1831), 1:20.

3. Saint Anselm, *St. Anselm's Proslogion: With a Reply on Behalf of the Fool by Gaunilo* (Oxford: Clarendon Press, 1965).

4. G. Douglass Lewis and Lovett Weems Jr., *A Handbook for Seminary Presidents* (Grand Rapids: Eerdmans, 2006).

5. Kathleen D. Billman and Bruce C. Birch, *C(H)AOS Theory: Reflections of Chief Academic Officers in Theological Education* (Grand Rapids: Eerdmans, 2011).

6. Wesley, "Sermon CXX—Causes of the Inefficacy of Christianity," in *The Works of the Rev. John Wesley, A.M.*, ed. John Emory (New York: Carlton & Lanahan, 1831), 2:441.

7. Ritual #829, *The Book of the United Methodist Hymns: Official Hymnal of The United Methodist Church* (Nashville: Board of Publication of The United Methodist Church, 1966).

8. William Farley Smith, "There Is a Balm in Gilead," adapted and arranged, 1986.

9. Edwin H. Friedman, *A Failure of Nerve: Leadership in the Age of the Quick Fix* (New York: Seabury Books, 2007), 53.

10. Robert K. Greenleaf, *Servant Leadership: A Journey into the Nature of Legitimate Power and Greatness* (Mahwah, NJ: Paulist Press, 1977), 49.

11. David Hempton, *Methodism: Empire of the Spirit* (New Haven, CT: Yale University Press, 2006), 52.

# 1. It's Just Not Working Anymore

1. We have been shrinking as a percentage of the United States population since the 1870s. Membership has been declining since 1967, and weekly worship attendance has dropped steadily since six weeks after September 11, 2001. Lovett H. Weems Jr., "No Shows: The Decline in Worship Attendance," *The Christian Century*, September 22, 2010.

2. Lovett H. Weems Jr., *Focus: The Real Challenges That Face The United Methodist Church* (Nashville: Abingdon, 2012). In the last five years, we have lost 3 percent of our congregations and 9 percent of our average weekly worship attendance.

3. Princeton, Yale, and Fuller are some of the most well-known examples.

4. Candler, Duke, Perkins, Boston, Garrett-Evangelical, Drew, and Wesley.

5. Of the total MEF apportionment, 25 percent is sent to annual conferences, and some is retained by the General Board of Higher Education. The remainder finds its way to the seminaries.

6. For example, Wesley produced, through our Wesley Ministry Network, a set of video-based courses for adult education in congregations. Over 200,000 people have taken these courses, but we lost money with each sale. Faculty received no royalties for their work. It was possible only because capital gifts were raised for the up-front production costs.

7. Jim Collins, *Good to Great: Why Some Companies Make the Leap . . . and Others Don't* (New York: HarperCollins, 2001).

8. Jim Collins, *How the Mighty Fall: And Why Some Companies Never Give In* (New York: HarperCollins, 2009), 20.

9. The following are the major studies and reflections on theological education, not otherwise cited, which are background sources for my observation about the nature and history of theological education in general and Methodist theological education in particular. They are listed in chronological order.

Kelly, Robert L. *Theological Education in America: A Study of One Hundred Sixty-One Theological Schools in the United States and Canada.* New York: George H. Doran Co., 1924.

Brown, William Adams, Charlotte V. Feeney, R. B. Montgomery, and Frank Shuttleworth, eds. *The Education of American Ministers.* New York: Institute of Social and Religious Research, 1934.

Niebuhr, H. Richard. *The Purpose of the Church and Its Ministry: Reflections on the Aims of Theological Education.* New York: Harper and Row, 1956.

Niebuhr, H. Richard, Daniel Day Williams, and James M. Gustafson, eds. *The Advancement of Theological Education: The Summary Report of a Mid-century Study.* New York: Harper & Brothers, 1957.

Gross, John O. "The Methodist Church and Theological Education." In *The Ministry in the Methodist Heritage*, ed. Gerald O. McCulloh. Nashville: Board of Education, The Methodist Church, 1960.

Deem, Warren. *Theological Education in the 1970s: A Report of the Resources Planning Commission.* Dayton, OH: Association of Theological Schools, 1968.

McCulloh, Gerald O. *Ministerial Education in the American Methodist Movement.* Nashville: United Methodist Board of Higher Education and Ministry, 1980.

Farley, Edward. *Theologia: The Fragmentation and Unity of Theological Education.* Philadelphia: Fortress, 1983.

Hough, Joseph C. and John B. Cobb Jr. *Christian Identity and Theological Education.* Chico, CA: Scholars Press, 1985.

Frazier, James W. *Schooling the Preachers: The Development of Protestant Theological Education in the United States, 1740–1875.* New York: University Press of America, 1988.

Miller, Glenn T. *Piety and Intellect: The Aims and Purposes of Antebellum Theological Education.* Atlanta: Scholars Press, 1990.

Kelsey, David H. *To Understand God Truly: What's Theological About a Theological School.* Louisville: Westminster/John Knox, 1992.

Pacala, Leon. *The Role of ATS in Theological Education 1980–1990.* Atlanta: Scholars Press, 1998.

Cannell, Linda. *Theological Education Matters: Leadership Education for the Church.* Newburgh, IN: EDCOT Press, 2006.

Aleshire, Daniel O. *Earthen Vessels: Hopeful Reflections on the Work and Future of Theological Schools.* Grand Rapids: Eerdmans, 2008.

Richey, Russell E. *Formation for Ministry in American Methodism: Twenty-First Century Challenges and Two Centuries of Problem-Solving.* Nashville: General Board of Higher Education and Ministry, 2014.

10. William Page Roberts, *Liberalism in Religion: And Other Sermons* (London: Smith, Elder & Co, 1886), vii.

# 2. Why It Matters

1. Lovett Weems Jr., "Ten Provocative Questions for the United Methodist Church" (presentation, Lake Junaluska, NC, November 5, 2007).

2. Ibid.

3. David Hempton, *Methodism: Empire of the Spirit* (New Haven, CT: Yale University Press, 2006), 57.

4. Randy Maddox, *Responsible Grace: John Wesley's Practical Theology* (Nashville: Kingswood Books, 1994), 38.

5. John Wesley, "The Character of a Methodist," in *The Works of the Rev. John Wesley, A.M.*, ed. John Emory (New York: Carlton & Lanahan, 1831), 5:240–48.

6. Ibid., "Thoughts Upon Methodism" (7:315).

7. Charles Wesley, "I Want a Principle Within," 1749.

8. John Wesley, "The Good Steward," in *The Works of the Rev. John Wesley, A.M.,* ed. John Emory (New York: Carlton & Lanahan, 1831), 1:451.

9. Maddox, *Responsible Grace*, 5; See Thomas A. Langford, *Practical Divinity: Theology in the Wesleyan Tradition* (Nashville: Abingdon, 1983).

10. John Wesley, *Primitive Physic: Or an Easy, Natural Method of Curing Most Diseases* (UK: Foundry & Moorfields, 1785).

11. Gary Chapman, *The Five Love Languages: How to Express Heartfelt Commitment to Your Mate* (Chicago: Northfield, 1995).

12. Maddox, *Responsible Grace*, 235–39.

13. Lester Ruth, *Early Methodist Life and Spirituality: A Reader* (Nashville: Kingswood Books, 2005), 37.

14. Myers-Brigg Type Indicator: http://www.myersbriggs.org.

15. *Silence of the Lambs*, directed by Jonathan Demme (Los Angeles: Orion Pictures, 1991).

16. Wesley, "The Scripture Way of Salvation," in *The Works of the Rev. John Wesley, A.M.,* ed. John Emory (New York: Carlton & Lanahan, 1831), 1:384–85.

17. Ibid., "The Way to the Kingdom" (1:64).

18. Bill Shore, *The Cathedral Within: Transforming Your Life by Giving Something Back* (New York: Random House, 2007).

# 3. Call the Question

1. David Field, *Bid Our Jarring Conflicts Cease: A Wesleyan Theology and Praxis of Church Unity* (Nashville: Foundry Books, 2017), xiv.

2. John Wesley, "Letter to Alexander Mather," August 6, 1777, *The Letters of the Rev. John Wesley,* ed. John Telford (London: Epworth Press, 1931), VI:272.

3. After his services as Wesley Seminary Board chair ended and after a life in the private practice of law, Steve now serves as the General Counsel of GCFA, the nearest thing we have to a General Counsel for The United Methodist Church. He is referring to Paragraph 120 of the 2016 *Book of Discipline.*

4. Ronald A. Heifetz and Marty Linsky, *Leadership on the Line: Staying Alive through the Dangers of Leading* (Boston: Harvard Business School Publishing, 2002).

5. Robert Lear, May 13, 2000, GC 081, "United Methodists Wrap up 2000 General Conference," http://gc2000.org /gc2000news/stories/gc081.htm. (Robert is the former head of the United Methodists News Service.)

6. J. Richard Peck, May 6, 2008, "General Conference Acts on Wide Range of Issues," http://www.umc.org/news-and-media /general-conference-acts-on-wide-range-of-issues.

7. James C. Collins and Jerry I. Porras, "Big Hairy Audacious Goals," *Built to Last: Successful Habits of Visionary Companies* (New York: HarperBusiness 1994), 91–114.

8. Lovett H. Weems Jr., *Focus: The Real Challenges That Face the United Methodist Church* (Nashville: Abingdon, 2011), 8.

9. Details of this project, including the results of research on thousands of pastors, can be found at www.wellbeing.nd.edu /flourishing-in-ministry/.

10. Ibid.

11. Penny Long Marler, et al, *So Much Better: How Thousands of Pastors Help Each Other Thrive* (St. Louis: Chalice Press, 2013), 5.

12. Wesley's Lewis Center for Church Leadership offers such a course free online: https://www.churchleadership.com/clergy -personal-finance-resources/.

# 4. Disruptive Innovation

1. Clayton Christensen, *The Innovator's Solution* (Boston: Harvard Business School Press, 2003), 34.

2. The Mormon First Presidency and Brigham Young University faculty have agreed with my characterization of the Latter-Day Saints as "Methodists on steroids."

3. Kenda Creasy Dean, *Almost Christian: What the Faith of Our Teenagers Is Telling the American Church* (New York: Oxford University Press, 2010), 6.

4. Wesley, "Sermon II—The Almost Christian," in *The Works of the Rev. John Wesley, A.M.,* ed. John Emory (New York: Carlton & Lanahan, 1831), 1:20.

5. Jacqueline Howard, "Millennials More Conservative Than You Think," *CNN,* September 7, 2016, under "Health," http://www .cnn.com/2016/09/07/health/millennials-conservative-generations /index.html.

6. A good summary, Henry H. Knight, III, "Wesley on Faith and Good Works" is provided at http://www.catalystresources.org /wesley-on-faith-and-good-works/.

7. See Lesslie Newbigin, *Foolishness to the Greeks: The Gospel and Western Culture* (Grand Rapids: Eeermans, 1986). See also Darrell Guder, *Missional Church: A Vision for the Sending of the Church in North America* (Grand Rapids: Eerdmans, 1998).

8. Michael Frost and Alan Hirsch, *The Shaping of the Things to Come: Innovation and Mission for the Twenty-First–Century Church* (Peabody: Hendrickson, 2003).

9. *The Book of Discipline of The United Methodist Church, 2016* (Nashville: The United Methodist Publishing House, 2016), ¶120, 91.

10. F. Douglass Powe Jr., *New Wine New Wineskins: How African American Congregations Can Reach New Generations* (Nashville: Abingdon, 2012), 105.

11. See https://ministryincubators.com/.

# 5. Seminaries Are the Solution, Part 1

1. More information about "traditioned innovation" can be found at Duke Divinity's Leadership Education online magazine *Faith & Leadership* at www.faithandleadership.com.

2. Harry Emerson Fosdick, *God of Grace and God of Glory* (1930).

3. Max De Pree, *Leadership Is an Art* (New York: Dell Publishing, 1989), 22.

4. C. S. Lewis, *The Screwtape Letters with Screwtape Proposes a Toast* (San Francisco: Harper Collins), 161.

5. King received his PhD from Boston University and whose thesis advisor, L. Harold DeWolf, became Wesley's first dean.

6. Martin Luther King Jr., "Letter from a Birmingham Jail" (The Estate of Martin Luther King, Jr.; Martin Luther King, Jr. Papers Project, www.kingpapers.org)

7. Elizabeth Svoboda, *What Makes a Hero: The Surprising Science of Selflessness* (New York: Penguin, 2013), 8.

8. Sebastian Junger, *Tribe: On Homecoming and Belonging* (New York: Twelve, 2016), 124.

9. Edwin H. Friedman, *A Failure of Nerve: Leadership in the Age of the Quick Fix* (New York: Seabury Books, 2007), 14.

10. William H. Willimon, *Calling and Character: Virtues of the Ordained Life* (Nashville: Abingdon, 2000), 21.

11. Sathianathan Clarke, June 2017, e-mail message to author.

12. Good hybrid education does not save money. There is a lower student to faculty ratio but it requires significant hardware and software support. It is instructive that the largest companies offering online resources—Blackboard, Google, Microsoft, Amazon, Facebook—all have many physical corporate offices and hold regular face-to-face meetings.

# 6. Seminaries Are the Solution, Part 2

1. Dan Aleshire, "The Future Has Arrived: Changing Theological Education in a Changed World." Paper presented at the Association of Theological Schools/Commission on Accrediting Biennial Meeting, June 2010.

2. Available from www.cokesbury.com.

3. For example, Wesley Seminary produced a video series for adult study groups entitled "Religion and Science: Pathways to Truth." The host of the series is Dr. Francis S. Collins, now Director of the National Institutes of Health. The series includes conversations with two Nobel Laureates in physics and seminary

professors. One of the best thing that ever happened in my office was when Dr. Collins and one of the Nobel Laureates finished their taping one evening and played guitars and sang hymns together (that is an "extra" in that video series). Go to www.church leadership.com to purchase or download previously generated courses through the Wesley Ministry Network.

4. Professor Sathianathan Clarke, who occupies the Bishop Sundo Kim Chair in World Christianity, created an online course entitled "Passionately Christian, Compassionately Interfaith" as a demonstration of this approach. Massive Open Online Course (Washington, DC: Wesley Theological Seminary, 2016), www.bea disciple.com/wesley.

5. E. Brooks Holifield, *God's Ambassadors: A History of the Christian Clergy in America* (Grand Rapids: Eerdmans, 2007), 145–81.

6. Douglas M. Strong, *Perfectionist Politics: Abolitionism and the Religious Tensions of American Democracy* (Syracuse, NY: Syracuse University Press, 1999).

7. Sondra Wheeler, *The Minister as Moral Theologian: Ethical Dimensions of Pastoral Leadership* (Grand Rapids: Baker, 2017).

8. We have established a Center for Public Theology (CPT). Distinguished Professor of Public Theology Mike McCurry directs the Center. Former White House Press Secretary for the last four presidential elections, he was co-chair of the Commission on Presidential Debates. As one who once faced the White House press corps, McCurry is often called on by both spokespeople and the press to address the question: "How can we find ways to re-establish trust and civil discourse?" The CPT is developing resources for pastors and churches. We are also now a resource to our city, especially journalists, to better understand the ways faith and public life intersect. See https://www.wesleyseminary.edu/ice/programs/public-theology/.

9. Kyunglim Shin Lee, Chang Hyung Pac, and Deokjoo Rhie, *Missionary Power, Urgent Expression of Korean Mission* (Seoul, Korea: Hongsung Books, 2017).

10. Helmut Thielicke, *A Little Exercise for Young Theologians* (Grand Rapids: Eerdmans, 1962), 8.

11. The premier program is the Wabash Center for Teaching and Learning in Theology and Religion: https:/www.wabashcenter .wabash.edu.

12. Ann Michel, September 3, 2017, conversation with author.

13. For more information, visit https://www.lpli.org.

14. Malcolm Gladwell, *Outliers: The Story of Success* (New York: Little, Brown, 2008).

15. Justo Gonzalez, *The History of Theological Education* (Nashville: Abingdon, 2015), 139.

16. Elders and local pastors are appointed as pastors of congregations. Since at least the 1980s there has been major decline in the number of active elders, while the number of local pastors increased dramatically. Since 1990 there have been 7,355 fewer elders and 3,576 more local pastors. In 1990, there were over five elders for each local pastor; today, there are just under two elders per local pastor. In 2017, there are 14,152 elders and 7,512 local pastors. *Clergy Age Trends in The United Methodist Church, 2017 Report* (Washington, DC: Lewis Center for Church Leadership, Wesley Theological Seminary, 2017).

17. Visit www.churchleadership.com to see the range of resources already available.

18. Wesley has developed these resources. Visit www.bea disciple.com/wesley/ to participate and actively engage in online courses through the Wesley Theological Seminary Lay Academy. Go to www.churchleadership.com to purchase or download previously generated courses through the Wesley Ministry Network.

19. Kenneth H. Carter, "Reaching More People," presentation (Washington, DC: Wesley Theological Seminary, September 29, 2017).

20. Lew Parks, *Small on Purpose: Life in a Significant Church* (Nashville: Abingdon, 2017).

# 7. Assurance

1. Stephen R. Covey, *The 7 Habits of Highly Effective People: Powerful Lessons in Personal Change* (New York: Simon & Schuster, 1989), 102.

2. Henry H. Knight II, *The Presence of God in the Christian Life: John Wesley and the Means of Grace* (London: Scarecrow Press, 1992), 19.

3. In fact, in the version of the Bible Wesley read, the word *subsistence* is in place of *assurance;* nevertheless, he uses the word *assurance* to describe the experience.

CPSIA information can be obtained
at www.ICGtesting.com
Printed in the USA
LVOW13s2245020318
568536LV00001B/1/P